Dedication

To my sisters, who have been an inspiration, encouragement and joy to me. You've propelled me to be all I could be.
I love ya'll.

12 Sisters Who Changed History

Table of Contents

TABLE OF CONTENTS	1
DEDICATION	3
CHAPTER ONE INTRODUCTION	5
CHAPTER TWO ATHENA AND ARTEMIS	7
CHAPTER THREE RACHEL AND LEAH	17
CHAPTER FOUR TRU'NG TRAC AND TRU'NG NHI	37
CHAPTER FIVE MARY AND ANNE BOLEYN	43
CHAPTER SIX MARY AND ELIZABETH TUDOR	63
CHAPTER SEVEN SARAH AND ANGELINA GRIMKE	81
CHAPTER EIGHT CONCLUSION	103
THANK YOU FOR READING	106
FURTHER READING	107
OTHER BOOKS BY AMBER SCHAMEL	109

12 Sisters Who Changed History

© Copyright 2018 Vision Writer Publications & Amber Schamel
http://www.AmberSchamel.com
Published by Vision Writer Publications
200 S. Wilcox St. #328
Castle Rock, CO 80104
Print edition created 2018   ISBN 978-0-9991767-5-7

All rights reserved. No part of this publication may be reproduced, stored in a retrieval system, or transmitted in any form, or by any means –for example, electronic, photocopying, recording—without the prior written consent of the publisher. The only exception is brief quotations in printed reviews. Thank you for respecting the hard work of this author.

Cover design by Roseanna White Designs
Images of Athena and Artemis statues and map from Shutterstock

All Scriptures are taken from the King James Version (Public Domain)

Chapter One
Introduction

Throughout history, we have seen how one life can change nations, and even the world. From the Garden of Eden, when the decision of one person brought death upon the entire human race, to one man who invented a website that changed the way the world interacts, we see that a single life can bring great change. Think of Moses, who marched into Egypt and set a nation free. William Wilberforce, whose determination finally brought slavery in England to an end. Thomas Edison, whose inventive spirit brought light to dark night and created endless potential. The Wright brothers, who believed it was possible to fly and opened the door of possibility that led us all the way to the moon. History books are filled with such stories. But have you ever considered how a pair of sisters might change history?

In this study, we will meet twelve fascinating women who, united with—or against—their sister, forged nations, inspired governments, ruled the greatest nations of the time, and changed the course of history. We will discover not only the major events of their lives, but also the relationship they shared with their sister, and how that affected their influence.

Is it possible for a woman to sustain such an impact? Is it possible that sisters have the capability to build or destroy simply by their lives and relationships with each other?

History will tell. And perhaps, along the way, you will be challenged to assess what influence you and your sibling may bestow upon our world. And maybe…just maybe…you will find the vision to unite with your own family and take on the evils of the world.

Chapter Two
Athena and Artemis

Athena and Artemis (known to the Romans as Minerva and Diana) were the daughters of Zeus in Greek mythology. While these two figures are either legendary women whose deeds were stretched to extraordinary proportions or complete products of imagination, they did affect history, as we will see.

The Birth of Athena

Athena, considered the goddess of wisdom, handicraft, and war, was the principal deity of the Greek capital of Athens. Deep in the legends of Greek mythology, we find the story for which Athena is best known. The story of her...ahem...unusual birth.

1 Fresco Depiction of the Birth of Athena

2 Statue of Athena

As the story goes, her father—the mighty Zeus—was told that the child he fathered with Metis would be wiser and take the throne from him. This would be just punishment, since Zeus himself had taken the throne from his own father. Cronus, the father of Zeus, swallowed each of his own children after their birth, but Zeus took it one step further and swallowed pregnant Metis. Afterward, he developed a horrible headache from which he could find no relief. He suffered so much that he begged Hephaestus to split his head open to relieve the pressure. When Hephaestus obliged, Athena sprang fully grown, wearing weapons and armor, from the slit in his head. The image of a midwife wielding an axe to split Zeus's head was a popular theme in the art of the ancient Greeks. Athena was often associated with owls, a symbol of wisdom, and olive trees, the symbol of peace. In some accounts, her armor was said to be made of the skin of a giant, hung with tassels of gold.

Of course, such tales are of little interest to us today, except for the fact that they had a tremendous influence upon the Greeks as well as the Romans, who in turn influenced the entire world. Especially America. But we'll get to that in a moment.

According to the myth, Athena was Zeus's favorite child and had great power. She was even allowed to use her father's weapons, such as the thunderbolt. Athena was known as the virgin goddess, a warrior maiden and, therefore, had priestesses in her temples. She was widely worshiped but is most commonly remembered for the city of Athens, which emerged about the time that Greece went from monarchy to democracy. Her temple in Athens is one of the Seven Wonders of the Ancient World and was a religious hub for the Greeks.

Athena was also honored in several other Greek cities, including Sparta, Thebes, and Corinth. She was credited with many inventions, including the bridle—which gave humans the ability to tame horses—the ship, and the chariot. Greek mythology credits Athena with creating the very first spider when she went into a rage and cursed a prideful mortal, who then morphed into the awful insect.

The City of Athens

The city of Athens is mentioned in the Scriptures. In Acts chapter 17, Paul was visiting Athens when he noticed an inscription "to the unknown god." His heart was grieved for the idolatry of the people, and he delivered one of his most famous sermons there.

3 Athens Coin Depicting Athena

The city of Athens seemed to be an intricate piece in the development of democracy in Greece. In fact, some would say that Athens was the founder of democracy.[1] And it was this Greek form of democracy that greatly influenced the Founding Fathers when they set up the United States as a republic. Had it not been for this goddess, who was the "guardian of the city and inspired restraint and practical insight,"[2] in the people, Greece may never have become the world influence that it has.

> *"What Athens was in miniature, America will be in magnitude,"* ~Thomas Paine

Some of the regulations in American government can be traced directly back to Athens. For example, it was an Athenian custom for payment to be made to those who served on a jury or other such governmental services. The practice of having representatives from each area was also an Athenian idea.

The Birth of Artemis

Artemis, the huntress, was also known as Diana. Athena's half-sister, she and her twin brother, Apollo, were conceived through the infidelity of Zeus and Leto. Most accounts claim that Hera, the god's true wife, was so angry that she forbade Leto to give birth on solid ground and sent the giant snake Python to

---

[1] BBC History on Greek Democracy

[2] Cartwright, Mark. "Athena." Ancient History Encyclopedia. Ancient History Encyclopedia, 24 May 2012. Web. 29 Jun 2018. & http://www.goddess.ws/athena.html

chase her and make sure she did not. However, she was able to escape and gave birth on an island near Delos. While the Greek stories vary in facts, it is most commonly stated that Artemis was born first and then acted as midwife as her mother delivered her twin brother, Apollo. It is because of this myth that she was believed to be the goddess of fertility and an aid to women during childbirth. Like her sister Athena, Artemis was favored by Zeus, and while sitting on his knee one day, she asked him to grant her several wishes. One of those wishes was to remain a virgin. According to all the tales, she carefully guarded not only her virtue but that of her followers as well.

Not only was she was known as the goddess of nature and fertility, but she was also attributed with power over all forms of wildlife and even the moon. She was worshiped in Ephesus, in Sparta, on the island of Delos (near the island where she was supposedly born), in Attica at Brauron, and in Mounikhia, but she was well known in all of Greece. In Athens, young girls were sent to the temple of Artemis at Brauron to serve for one year before they reached puberty.

4 Statue of Artemis

The City of Ephesus

Artemis, or Diana, was the principal deity of Ephesus. The temple of Artemis in Ephesus was also one of the Seven Wonders of the Ancient World. The original temple of Artemis dates back to the 7th century BC. The temple was destroyed and rebuilt three times, which indicates that the site must have been considered sacred for an extended time. The sacredness of the site probably resulted from a meteor that struck the earth near that point. As mentioned in the book of Acts, the Ephesians believed that Diana's image "fell from the heavens."[3] This reference was to a great stone that appears to have been part of a meteorite. The people thought it looked like Diana and began worshiping it.

The last temple was set aflame by Goth raiders around AD 268[4] The shrine must have been grand, and the goddess held in great esteem among the people for her to be worshiped on that site for around 1,000 years. Of the 121 columns that comprised the third rebuilding of the temple, only one remains standing today.

So great was the influence of this goddess, especially in Ephesus, that the businessmen of the city became enraged when Christians began missionary work in the area. The Scriptures (in Acts 19) record the incident in which the silversmiths enrage the entire city against Paul for preaching against the goddess. They

---

[3] Acts 19:35

[4] History of the Goths by Thomas J. Dunlap, Wolfram Herwig p 52f

proclaim:

> *Sirs, ye know that by this craft we have our wealth.*
>
> *Moreover ye see and hear, that not alone at Ephesus, but almost throughout all Asia, this Paul hath persuaded and turned away much people, saying that they be no gods, which are made with hands:*
>
> *So that not only this our craft is in danger to be set at nought; but also that the temple of the great goddess Diana should be despised, and her magnificence should be destroyed, whom all Asia and the world worshippeth. (Acts 19:25-27)*

5 Ephesian Coin Depicting Artemis

"Whom all Asia and the world worships"? So then, the influence of this mythical woman must have been great at the time. Some scholars also argue that Artemis was a "savior goddess," which would have made the preaching of Christ as Savior even more offensive to the Ephesians. Still, many in Ephesus were converted to the truth, and one of the epistles recorded in the Holy Scriptures is addressed to them.

In more current times, she is considered the "feminist goddess" and is used to fuel the fires of many feminist ideas. This stems mostly from the way Artemis was a feminine goddess with her gifts of fertility and charm, however she also filled more masculine roles such as hunter and savior, but also from her nature of being completely independent of men. She needed not their approval, nor their companionship. Artemis inspires feminists in today's society to be "independent, strong, to trust our instincts & intuitions, and to love and understand the wild and vulnerable around us and inside us."[5]

History Remembers

From this study, we see that these two sisters—while they were mythical—still affected the culture of ancient times and even beyond. They generated commerce, inspired the building of temples that were icons of engineering and architecture, dictated the lives of those who worshiped them, influenced people's thinking, and had cities dedicated to them that later became chief

---

[5] *Artemis: Her many Faces* by Katharina Woodworth

locations in the Christian movement.

If a "legend" or imaginary character can do that, what more could you and I?

12 Sisters Who Changed History

Chapter Three
Rachel and Leah

We all remember the Bible story of Rachel and Leah, but have you ever thought about their lasting impact? It's remarkable.

Leah and Rachel were raised in "the land of the people of the east" according to Genesis 29. The exact location this refers to is unknown, but it was in the country that was then known as Mesopotamia, which corresponds mostly with modern-day Iraq. The girls were the daughters of Rebekah's brother Laban, so they would have been first cousins to Jacob, whose mother was Laban's sister.

6 Dante's Rachel & Leah

As Jacob fled from the wrath of his brother, Esau, after having tricked him into giving up his birthright, he sought out his uncle Laban, in the land of Haran. He noticed a group of shepherds gathered at the community well and stopped to rest and speak with them. They all knew his uncle and told him that if he would wait a few moments, the man's daughter would appear, because she cared for his sheep. The fact that Rachel held this occupation is interesting, especially since her father seemed to have many servants.

Even as the men spoke of her, Rachel appeared. Jacob's cousin turned out to be lovely, and Jacob was immediately struck by her beauty. He greeted her with a kiss and rolled the stone away from the mouth of the well so she could water her flock. This kiss has been the subject of much controversy over the years. John Calvin believed Moses, in writing the account, must have inverted the order of the scene. In his Bible commentary, Calvin asserted that Jacob did not kiss her until after he had informed her that he was her cousin,[6] for Calvin did not want to give anyone an excuse for such immodesty. Other scholars, such as Matthew Henry deemed it "kisses of love," for Jacob was smitten with her "ingenuous comely face."[7] Hebrew scholars have deemed it a formal greeting, although offered with deep emotion.[8] Whichever

---

[6] Genesis 29 Commentary by John Calvin

[7] Genesis 29 Commentary by Matthew Henry

it was, it sent Rachel running home to her father.

I wonder what Leah's reaction was when Rachel came running home one afternoon, excitedly telling her father that she'd found a long-lost relative of theirs at the well. What might have been the sisters' thoughts as their father ran out to meet him and invited him to stay?

The scene surely struck a familiar memory for Laban, because years before his sister had run home from the well with a similar story. He must have thought, "What is it about Abraham's family and asking for the first woman they meet at the well?" Perhaps the similarities between his parents' love story and his meeting this beautiful girl was influential for Jacob. But he had no lavish gifts to present to Laban, as Eliezer had.

Some scholars believe Jacob to have been around seventy-seven years old at this time, and while we don't know Rachel's or Leah's ages, the fact that they were both yet unmarried would imply that they were very young.

The Bible introduces the elder sister, Leah, as being "tender eyed." The meaning of this phrase is debatable; however, it is commonly assumed that it suggests something unattractive about her eyes as the Scripture goes on to say, "but Rachel was beautiful and well favoured"[9].

I came across another explanation suggesting that since Laban

---

[8] The Torah: A Modern Commentary by W. Gunther Plaut page 199

[9] Genesis 29:17

had two daughters and his sister Rebekah had two sons, it was assumed that the four would make two couples. Leah would marry Esau, and Rachel would marry Jacob. Knowing the character of the elder brother, Leah may have spent most of her young life in prayerful tears begging God to change her destined fate. Thus her eyes were soft or weary from weeping.

Whatever the cause, Jacob favored Rachel and fell deeply in love with her. He was even willing to work seven years for her with apparently no other compensation.

Laban was a man of standing in Haran, and one who was fluent in the laws of his people. This is made clear by his agreements and conduct with Jacob. Every time Jacob tried to make a move, Laban was there with a law or custom that dictated what Jacob could or couldn't do. Whether his knowledge of the laws and customs was legitimate, or whether he used them to manipulate his naïve nephew is unclear.

When Jacob approached Laban about working to earn Rachel's hand in marriage, Laban seemed agreeable. During those days, it was a common occurrence for a laborer to exchange his service for a percentage of the flock, or some similar agreement. So this proposition was not far off the norm. Jacob and Laban made a deal, and Jacob fulfilled his side of the bargain. Seven years of hard labor in exchange for the beautiful Rachel. This didn't bother Jacob at all, for the Bible tells us that the first seven years "seemed but a few days, for the love he had to her"[10].

A Wedding Surprise

When the contract term was fulfilled, Laban's family threw a wedding feast for Jacob and his bride. Somehow or another, Laban caused Leah, rather than Rachel, to be brought into Jacob. Tradition holds that Leah was heavily veiled, and thus the scheme was not discovered until the morning. Due to this account, it is Jewish tradition for the groom to veil the bride himself shortly before the wedding ceremony, to ensure he is marrying the right bride.

When Jacob confronted his uncle about the situation, what was Laban's defense? He claimed it was due to the custom for the elder sister to marry first. The Matthew Henry commentaries deny that there was any fact to back up Laban's claim. Regardless, Laban got what he wanted; another seven years of labor out of Jacob.

It is hard to imagine what family relations must have been like during those years. Jacob and Rachel in love, but Leah standing in the place as Jacob's rightful wife, and Laban's deceit the cause of the whole thing.

I have often wondered what Leah's feelings were throughout the drama. Later in the text we see her wishing for her husband to

---

[10] Genesis 29:20

love her, trying to earn his favor by giving him many sons. Did she get a taste of that love during the seven years she had Jacob to herself? Did she love him before their marriage? Was she a part of Laban's deception in marrying her off to Jacob first, or was she pressed into it? These are questions we can never know the answer to.

When the second set of seven years' labor was accomplished, Rachel finally wed Jacob. The Scriptures give us a glimpse into Leah's life at this time in Genesis 29:30-31, telling us that Jacob loved Rachel more than Leah. That phrase would indicate that perhaps Jacob did care for Leah and treated her well enough, but Rachel was his prize. Rachel was the one he loved.

Rachel, Favored by Jacob, Leah, Favored by God

It is interesting that Leah seems to have been barren during the first seven years, because the Scriptures tell us that because she was hated, God opened her womb. Hated? By whom? Jacob or her sister? The Hebrew word translated "hated" is also translated as "enemy, foe, utterly hate, or odious." A strong word. So did Jacob hate her and only fulfil his duty to her out of obligation because he was honorable?

Leah recognized her fruitfulness as God's favor, for when she gave birth to her firstborn son, she named him Reuben, which means "see, a son." But her comment is even more striking:

> For she said, Surely the Lord hath looked upon
> my affliction; now therefore my husband will love
> me. (Genesis 29:32b)

Leah now has the upper hand because she has produced an heir for Jacob. Perhaps now her desire, just to be loved by her own husband, will be fulfilled. Whatever Rachel and Leah's relationship had been before Jacob arrived in Haran, it was now headed downhill. Fast.

I must confess that before I began my in-depth study of these sisters, my thoughts favored Rachel. She is the one portrayed as the caring, beautiful, and favored mother. The one who was cheated out of her marriage and then struggled to have the children she always wanted. The heart of a mother "weeping for her children." But as I explored the scriptural texts and the historical commentaries, it has shed light on Rachel's many weaknesses and on Leah's quiet strengths.

Here we find this beautiful story of Leah's struggle, her initial barrenness, the rejection of not only her husband, but also her sister and father. Yet throughout this trial that would span much of her life, we do not see her upbraiding her husband for his fault. Instead, we see her in a humble and grateful attitude thanking God for His favor. The respect and regard toward both God and her husband is reflected in the names she chose for her sons. She didn't blame God for her situation, which would have been easy to do. Instead, she thanks God for His aid and support. Here is God being a favorable lover to her when she lacked one.

Apparently giving Jacob his firstborn son didn't bring his favor as she hoped, because the next son born to Leah she named Simeon, which in Hebrew means "heard." She declares, "Because the Lord has heard that I was hated, He has given me this son also."

Not long after, God blessed her with a third son, Levi, meaning "joined." She believed that now her husband would be joined to her since she had given him three healthy sons. The Hebrew word translated as "joined" can also mean "to abide" or "to cleave." Leah was desirous that her husband would "cleave to her" as his wife.

But when Leah's fourth son came along, her attitude seems to have changed. His name, Judah, means "praise." It is no longer about her husband's favor; instead, she is letting go and saying, "Now will I praise the Lord."

We can learn a lot from Leah's example. When our hopes and dreams are shattered, casting fault and blame upon God will do us no good. If we are faithful, God will comfort us. But in the end, it is surrender and lifting our hands in praise to God that will bring us peace.

Whatever we have that contributes either to our support and comfort under our afflictions, or to our deliverance from them, God must be owned in it. ~ Matthew Henry[11]

---

[11] Genesis 29 Commentary by Matthew Henry

After the fourth son, God again closed Leah's womb. But this didn't keep Rachel from becoming envious.

Jacob's mother, Rebekah, also struggled with barrenness, but it did not make her bitter. Jacob must have been surprised at the effect it had on Rachel, being from the same family as his mother, but so different in her response. In her anger, Rachel lashed out at her husband saying, "Give me children, else I die!" This angered Jacob, and he sent back a scathing response, "Do you think I am God? That it is I who withholds children from you?"

Ouch. Jacob reminded her that it wasn't he who was the problem. He had fathered four sons. It was her womb, she was the "problem." True, she had Jacob's favor, but not God's. In this, Leah was happier than Rachel.

Again, what a stark contrast between the attitudes of the two sisters. Both of them hungered for favor they lacked, Leah for Jacob's, and Rachel for God's. Leah responded with a spirit of humble gratitude and respect, while Rachel responded in a spirit of anger and bitterness. It was Rachel's attitude that fueled the next round of conflict in their family.

The Childbearing War Begins

After claiming she would die because of her anguish, Rachel begged Jacob to take her maid, Bilhah, so that she could bear children on Rachel's behalf. To us today, this seems like an odd request, but in those days, it was not uncommon to have a bondwoman bear the child—serving almost as a surrogate—and then the mistress would adopt the babe as her own. Jacob consented to this plan, and Bilhah gave birth to a son.

> *And Rachel said, God hath judged me, and hath also heard my voice, and hath given me a son; therefore, called she his name Dan. (Genesis 30:6)*

What was it that Rachel believed God would judge her for? Did she think she was in the wrong for something? Until now, it seems Rachel had felt like the victim. So why the sudden change? The Bible gives us yet another glimpse into the sisters' relationship a few verses later.

The maid-bearing saga continued with Rachel's maid having another son, and then Leah following suit by offering her own maid to Jacob, and she also bore two sons. Jacob now had eight sons by four women, still the madness continued.

Rueben, Leah's eldest son, found mandrakes, an herb that was considered to aid in conceiving a child, in the field. He brought the herb to his mother, but when Rachel found out about it, she confronted her sister and requested she give it to her. Leah's impertinent reply, and the resulting bargain, reveal much about their conflict:

> *Is it a small matter that thou hast taken my husband? and wouldest thou take away my son's mandrakes also? (Genesis 30:15)*

Leah accused Rachel of taking her husband. But isn't that

backward? Leah is the one that was deceitfully given to Jacob instead of Rachel. So how could she make such a claim? But Rachel doesn't deny it. Instead, she makes a deal. Jacob will spend the night with Leah in exchange for the herb. When Jacob returns from the field, Leah greets him by telling him he must come to her, for she has "hired" him in exchange for the herb. This situation implies that Leah was not often with Jacob. Now, Rachel's guilty conscience and Leah's claim that Rachel stole her husband falls into place. God again favored Leah, and she conceived another son, Issachar.

She must have found a way around her sister's demands again, because she also bore a sixth son, whom she named Zebulun, saying, "God hath endued me with a good dowry; now will my husband dwell with me, because I have born him six sons".[12] Apparently, things improved, because she later bore a daughter as well.

Perhaps over the years Rachel was able to work through her bitterness and find some measure of peace, because at last, God remembered Rachel and opened her womb as well. She brought forth a son and named him Joseph. Her gratitude is shown here, as she thanks the Lord for taking away her reproach.

Leaving Haran

Now with eleven sons and a daughter, Jacob was ready to

---

[12] Genesis 30:20

leave Haran. He spoke with Laban and requested permission to leave, taking his wife and children with him. Laban begged him to stay, and they worked out a contract so that Jacob would earn a portion of the flock for his labor. However, this agreement doesn't satisfy Laban for very long, because when he saw how much God prospered Jacob, he changed the deal. Several times, Jacob tolerated the shifting of contract, but when Laban's sons started murmuring against Jacob, and he could see Laban's attitude toward him had changed, he decided it was time to leave.

He called Rachel and Leah into the field and recounted to them a dream that he'd been given from God. The Lord saw all that Laban had done to him, changing his wages ten times, and he prospered Jacob. But in the dream, the angel of the Lord told him to leave. His wives responded, saying that they, too, had lost favor with their father and that he had squandered anything that might have been their inheritance. The two sisters had enough harmony between them to support their husband. "Whatsoever God hath said unto thee, do."

Rachel's Theft

Unbeknownst to Laban, Jacob packed up his family, servants, cattle and all that he had and fled to Canaan. It seems the sisters were ready for a change. Life in Haran had been difficult, between the conflict between themselves and the conflict with their father and brothers. Perhaps they believed going to Jacob's family in Canaan would be a new start for them. Rachel, however, must have longed to keep something from her homeland, because she took her father's idols and stashed them among her things as they fled.

7Rachel Sitting Upon the Idols

The significance of the idols and Rachel's motivation for taking them have been a subject of heavy debate amongst scholars. Some believe the idols were a means of divination and that Rachel was afraid Laban would use them to discover their plans. Others claim she wanted her father to give up his pagan ways and stole the idols so that he could no longer worship them. Still others maintain that the idols were believed to provide protection, which would explain Rachel's need of them, and also Laban's fury at being left unprotected. The Nuzi records indicate that the idols were a symbol of property rights and family status, the "keys to the house" so to speak.[13] Perhaps Rachel believed the

---

[13] The Torah: A Modern Commentary by W. Gunther Plaut page 214

title to the estate was rightfully theirs between Jacob's labors and his marriage to two of their family members.

The most likely explanation is that the idols were valuable, and she took them for that reason. Perhaps she wanted something they could sell if all their flocks perished during the journey. Or perhaps she believed they could be used to charm Esau as he and Jacob made amends. Whatever the cause, she took them, but kept it a secret from her husband. And it wasn't long before her father noticed that they were missing.

It must have been spring when the family set out to leave, because the Scriptures mention it was the time of sheep shearing. In fact, it was this sheep shearing season that made Laban realize that Jacob and his family were gone.

Sheep shearing was a major event in ancient Mesopotamia. Many cities had lavish religious services and festivals during this season. Laban's company must have participated in something similar, because it was during the time of sheep shearing that he realized his idols were missing. It was then that his servants told him that Jacob had fled, three days past. Whether someone had seen Rachel take the idols, or if they believed Jacob would have taken them because they did indeed hold some sort of inheritance rights, we don't know.

Gathering his brethren together, Laban lit out after his son-in-law, who he believed had taken not only his daughters and grandchildren, but also his cherished idols. For a full week, Laban pursued Jacob, but right before he caught up to them, God visited Laban in a dream. Laban was warned to say nothing good or bad to Jacob, but to be careful in how he addressed him.

Jacob had just reached Mount Gilead when Laban overtook him.

> *And Laban said to Jacob, What hast thou done, that thou hast stolen away unawares to me, and carried away my daughters, as captives taken with the sword? Wherefore didst thou flee away secretly, and steal away from me; and didst not tell me, that I might have sent thee away with mirth, and with songs, with tabret and with harp? And hast not suffered me to kiss my sons and my daughters? Thou hast now done foolishly in so doing. (Gen. 31:26-28)*

While these words sound sentimental and ridden with justifiable hurt, with Laban's threat of violence, one must wonder whether they were true words or merely manipulative. Was he giving Jacob a guilt trip when all he really cared about was getting his idols back? Or did he intend to kill Jacob in order to keep the rest of his family in Haran? It's unclear what is meant by Laban's remark of "it is in the power of my hand to do thee hurt," but it was only because of the dream that he stayed his hand.

Jacob responds by admitting that he was afraid Laban would take Rachel and Leah away from him by force. When the conversation turns to the theft of the idols, Jacob makes a bold oath to Laban, not knowing his favored wife was the thief.

12 Sisters Who Changed History

> *With whomsoever thou findest thy gods, let him not live: before our brethren discern thou what is thine with me, and take it to thee. (Gen. 31:32)*

The search began. Laban entered each tent, searching for the idols. Rachel managed to hide them in a cushion of camel's hair that was used by women during their time of menstruation. She sat upon it, claiming she could not get up because the "custom of the women" was upon her. While she managed to hide the idols from her father, did she really escape Jacob's oath?

After covenanting with Laban and the emotional reunion with Esau, Jacob settled in Shechem near a city called Shalem. The family dwelt there for a time, and while God again opened Rachel's womb, trouble seemed to follow them wherever they went.

Leah's only daughter, Dinah, went into the city alone to visit the young women. While there, a prince of the city saw her, took her into his house, and defiled her. Even though the prince followed up by asking for Dinah's hand in marriage, Dinah's brothers were enraged. How dare this uncircumcised heathen do such a thing to their sister? And to give her in marriage to such a man would defile their tribes. Taking after the cunning natures of their father and grandfather Laban, Jacob's sons devised a plan. In order for this prince to gain permission to marry Dinah, he and his men would have to be circumcised. When the men were still weak from the procedure, two of Dinah's brothers, Simeon and Levi, fell upon them with swords, killed all the men, and took

Dinah back home.

Their actions troubled Jacob. How could they continue to dwell in the land, when the people would avenge the prince of Shechem? But Simeon and Levi remained unashamed. "Should we allow him to treat our sister as a harlot?"

Rachel's Death

God again visited Jacob, telling him to take his family to Bethel, near where he had reunited with Esau, and there build an altar. In preparation for this journey, Jacob declared a time of purification. They were to wash themselves and put away all strange gods from among them. He gathered all the pagan images and all of the earrings from their ears and buried them under an oak tree. Perhaps this is the point where Rachel's possession of her father's idols came to light.

At this time, Rachel was close to delivery of her second child. During the journey, she went into labor. It was a very hard birth, and Rachel barely delivered the child alive. With her dying breath, she gave her son a name: Ben-Oni, which means "son of my suffering," but some Hebrew scholars believe it is more accurately translated "son of my iniquity." Could it be that Jacob's curse upon the thief of Laban's idols had at last caught up to her? What makes this even more interesting is that Jacob did not leave his son with the name his favored wife gave him during her final breath. He altered the name to "Ben-Yamin," translated "son of my right hand" or more particularly, "son of my oath."

Therefore, Benjamin became the only son that Jacob named, for all the others had been named by either Leah or Rachel.

Jacob's oath that whoever was found with Laban's idols would not live came down upon the head of the one he loved most.

Rachel was buried beside the road in Ephrath, or Bethlehem. She was the only member of Jacob's family not buried in the ancestral tomb, which begs the question, why did Jacob not take his favorite wife to the place where he would be buried? Did God tell him not to turn back but to continue to Bethel? One Hebrew scholar presents the following opinion.

> *Why did Jacob bury Rachel in Ephrath?*
> *Because he saw a vision that all the exiles would*
> *pass by there, and he buried her along the road so*
> *she could weep and plead for mercy for her exiled*
> *children. (Chaim Potok, Hebrew scholar)*[14]

Whether that is true or not, we don't know. But it would explain the oddity.

---

[14] Wanderings: Chaim Potok's history of the Jews page 319

12 Sisters Who Changed History

8 Fresco of Rachel Weeping for her children

Leah's Death

What became of Leah after Rachel's death? The Scriptures do not mention the elder sister again until Jacob's death. When Jacob asks Joseph to swear not to bury him in Egypt, but take him to his ancestral tomb, he mentions that he buried Leah there. So while we know where Leah is buried, we do not know how or when she died. Could it be that she finally got the love and attention she craved after Rachel's death? Did she get to see her grandchildren? I wish we knew. The lack of record is heartbreaking.

History Remembers

What we do find in the record is how these two sisters changed the course of history. Their story and family relations are recorded the Scriptures, which have influenced millions of Jews and Christians alike. Many of the Jewish wedding customs and laws stem from their story. After the Israelites were brought out of Egypt, their laws banned marriages like the fiasco that was created by Laban's trickery.

Rachel gave birth to only two sons, Joseph and Benjamin, but her legacy was great as well. Joseph ascended to the right hand of Pharaoh in Egypt and managed to save not only the Egyptian people from famine but also countless others, including his own family, who became the nation of Israel.

Through the tribe of Benjamin came Hadassah, who became Queen Esther, yet another savior of Israel. King Saul, Gideon, and the apostle Paul were also her descendants. As for Rachel herself, she is remembered in history as a devout mother, thus the Scriptures describe "Rachel weeping for her children" in the day that Herod the Great destroyed the baby boys of Bethlehem.

What is most interesting to note is how each of these women plays a part in the birth of Jesus Christ. While the Messiah comes through the line of Judah, Leah's son, He is born in Bethlehem, Rachel's city and burial place. Somehow, through all of their bickering and feuds during their lifetime, God brings them together after their deaths in yet another important event in history. Surely this story was written by a Great Author.

Chapter Four
Tru'ng Trac and Tru'ng Nhi

Our next set of sisters takes us to Vietnam during the first century A.D. These two gals could be described as the Asian version of Joan of Arc. They lived during a time of great unrest in Vietnam, when the lords of China still ruled over them. But it was a pair of sisters who would lead the first major rebellion in favor of Vietnamese independence.

9 Statue of Tru'ng Sisters

Tru'ng Trac and her younger sister, Tru'ng Nhi, were born to a military family in Gaio Chi (northern Vietnam) during the Han Dynasty. With their father being the prefect of the region, the two girls were made to study martial arts and war strategy, which they would utilize later in life.

At some point, a neighboring prefect came to visit the Tru'ng girls' father. During this visit, the neighboring prefect's son, Thi Sach, met and fell in love with the eldest daughter. Soon a marriage was arranged.

The Execution of Tru'ng Trac's Husband

According to the Vietnamese accounts, the Han Dynasty was a difficult time for the oppressed people. The Chinese overlords were cruel and heartless. Fertile land was seized from noble families and bestowed upon Chinese immigrants, while hefty tributes and taxes were exacted from the Vietnamese people. Tru'ng Trac's husband made a stand against the Chinese and was executed. The overlords hoped to make an example of him and discourage further rebellion.

It backfired.

The *Book of the Later Han,* a chronicle of the era, describes Tru'ng Trac as a "ferocious warrior."[15] Apparently, this was true, because few women could have accomplished what happened next.

A Revolution of Women

Tru'ng Trac was rightfully enraged. She and her sister banded together around 40 A.D. and took over the revolutionary

---

[15] Book of the Later Han by Fan Ye

movement. They somehow managed to raise a fighting force, which seems to have been composed mostly of women. They marched on the commandery capital of Lien Lau and were victorious. The Chinese commander fled for his life. Vietnamese historians described it this way:

> *In the spring, the second month, the governor of Wangku Commandery, Tô Định, punished her [Tru'ng Trac] under the law, and she also hated Định for having killed her husband. She, therefore, along with her sister Nhị, rose and captured the commandery capital. ~Annals of Dai Viet*

It is truly amazing that two women were able to raise an army. It is a phenomenon that has yet to be understood.

> *Trưng Trắc, Trưng Nhị are women, with a single cry led the prefectures of Cửu Chân, Nhật Nam, Hợp Phố, and 65 strongholds heed their call. They established a nation and proclaimed their rule as easily as their turning over their hands. It awakened all of us that we can be independent. ~Le Van Hu'u, Vietnamese historian and editor of the Annuls.*

As time went on, the sisters and their allies captured sixty-five cities. Tru'ng Trac and Tru'ng Nhi became co-reigning queens of the newly liberated state.[16] However, their success did not last long. The emperor of China would soon send a force to overthrow the Sister Queens and restore order to the empire.

The Chinese accounts obviously record this event much differently. There is no trace of cruelty or abuse of the Vietnamese people in their histories, and no mention of the execution of Tru'ng Trac's husband. Instead, they assert that the rebellion was due to the Vietnamese people's misunderstanding of the Han laws, and disliking them—a problem that the Chinese general swiftly rectified.

Downfall and Death of the Sister Queens

During the second year of the Tru'ng sister's reign, the Han emperor ordered his general Ma Yuan to gather boats, wagons, and supplies and lead an army to overthrow the two sisters. By the third year, Ma Yuan had reached Sui Mountain and the city of Lang Bac. There his large army engaged the queens' forces. Due to the lack of military training and the small size of her force, Tru'ng Trac withdrew her forces to the Jin River. This increased the already lurking doubt that a woman could win the war, and her forces scattered. The Tru'ng kingdom ended after only three years of freedom.

The records of Trac and Nhi's deaths contradict each other.

---

16 "Đại Việt Sử Ký Toàn Thư – Kỷ Thuộc Hán" (in Vietnamese). Institute of Social Studies Vietnam. 1993.

The Chinese accounts state that the sisters were killed by Ma Yuan, who sent their decapitated heads to the emperor as proof of their demise.[17] Vietnamese histories claim that the sisters committed suicide to avoid capture. The most popular claim is that the pair drowned themselves in the river, but one legend even claims that they vanished into the sky. Regardless, their lives were lost, and instead they became objects of worship among their people.

Their rebellion now squelched, Vietnam would not gain independence again for almost nine hundred years.

History Remembers

Tru'ng Trac and Tru'ng Nhi are emblems of freedom and are revered still today in Vietnam. In an area where societies are male-dominated, Vietnam stands out as unique in the respect toward women. The Tru'ng sisters are the reason why women are held in such high esteem and granted freedoms that neighboring societies withhold.[18] There are many temples erected in their honor, and every year the Vietnamese people hold a celebration with elephant parades to remember their valor. Even though they lived more than two thousand years ago, the sisters are considered

---

[17] *Yu, Yingshi (1986). Denis Twitchett; Michael Loewe, eds. Cambridge History of China: Volume I: the Ch'in and Han Empires, 221 B.C. – A.D. 220. Page 454*

[18] Trung Sisters Encyclopædia Britannica
https://www.britannica.com/topic/Trung-Sisters

national symbols. Their legacy inspires patriotism and freedom in the Vietnamese people.

10 Procession of elephants during Tru'ng remembrance parade

Chapter Five
Mary and Anne Boleyn

Mary and Anne Boleyn were born during treacherous and changing times. Although these two sisters weren't as close as the others we've been covering, their influence on history is just as strong.

Mary seems to have been the elder of the two, both children of Thomas Boleyn, the first Earl of Wiltshire, and his wife, Lady Elizabeth Howard. Thomas Boleyn had gained respect in the Tudor dynasty by supporting Henry VII, and his station only grew stronger under Henry VIII. He was an ambitious man with a family strategy of using marriages to gain social standing, a trait that seemed to pass on to his daughter Anne as well. Thomas was a knight, and one of the most trusted courtiers in King Henry VIII's circle. It was this influence that introduced the Boleyn daughters to the attentions of the king. By 1511, Sir Thomas Boleyn had become a "favorite" of King Henry and had many lucrative appointments and positions, including being named Sherriff of Kent for multiple years.[19]

Probably only two or three years older, Mary was brought up with Anne and their brothers George and Thomas in Kent, England. Their French governess prepared them for their later occupations as ladies in waiting to the French queen. Their

---

[19] Alison Weir, *Mary Boleyn: The Mistress of Kings* (New York: Ballantine Books, 2012).

education consisted of basic principles of math and history, but also included family genealogy, hunting, singing, and skills in running a household. Many of these accomplishments are what helped to make the pair popular in King Henry VIII's court.

Mary Sent to the French Court

Around the age of fifteen, Mary Boleyn was sent with Princess Mary, Henry VIII's youngest sister, as a maid-of-honor when she moved to Paris and became the wife of aging King Louis XII of France. Here, Mary's reputation seems to have suffered. She is thought to have become the subject of several affairs and the mistress to the succeeding king, Francis I, although some historians consider those reports to be exaggerated.

11 Mary Boleyn

In actuality, there seems to be only one vague piece of evidence that mentions an affair with Francis I, and no evidence that suggests she behaved in a way to gain a negative reputation while at the French court. The most convincing proof that something did transpire is the fact that Mary Tudor had the young woman dismissed from court, and she disappears from record for about five years.

While no one can know of a certainty where Mary Boleyn spent those years, some evidence suggests that she was sent away to either a convent or a noble family's home in the French countryside to further her education and be taught moral conduct.[20] If this is true, it would indicate that there had, indeed, been an incident that marred young Mary Boleyn's reputation, and her father worked hard to keep it quiet. Her mistress, Mary Tudor, now a French queen, would have reason to keep it quiet as well, since it would also reflect upon her.

Anne Rises to the Scene

Now let's sidestep for a moment and catch up with the younger sister. Anne's early life followed closely in her sister's footsteps, although she would step out of her shadow and earn herself a greater place in history books, outshining her older sister in the royal courts, and also in their family's affections. Anne went to the Netherlands when she was probably near eight years

---

[20] Ibid.

of age and was tutored in the house of Margaret of Austria, who was the Duchess of Savoy and regent of her nephew Charles, who would become the Holy Roman Emperor.

When Mary Boleyn joined Mary Tudor's entourage for her marriage to King Louis XII, Anne was also appointed a maid-of-honor and joined her sister in France. The fact that Sir Thomas was able to procure a position for both of his daughters in the wedding party speaks to his influence with King Henry. During this stint in France, the two sisters were together in Queen Mary's court. The French king died in January of 1515, only three months after the wedding, leaving Queen Mary a widow. The Boleyn sisters were present to witness the Queen's secret betrothal to the Duke of Suffolk. In fact, it is likely that they stood as witnesses to the secret ceremony in February of the same year. The marriage was considered scandalous, since it had not been sanctioned by King Henry. Perhaps this event left an impression on Mary Boleyn, who would later opt for a similar second marriage.

When Queen Mary returned with the duke to England, Mary disappears from the court records for a number of years. Anne stayed behind in France as a member of Queen Claude's household. Her life there would have been closely guarded in almost convent-like conditions, as Queen Claude was known for her piety and was often away from court due to her pregnancies.[21]

---

[21] See Claire Ridgeway, The Anne Boleyn Files, blog, 2018, and Weir, *Mary Boleyn*.

Anne served in this pious household for about seven years. Apparently, it was these years in France in which Anne developed her religious interests and convictions, as well as a distinctly French taste and charm.

12 Anne Boleyn

Around 1522, Anne was recalled to England, most likely due to the rising political tensions between the French and English kings; however, there seems to have been a second motive as well. A heated debate over land rights between Anne's father and her uncle threatened civil war. King Henry hoped to end the conflict by marrying her off to her Irish cousin, James Butler.[22] These plans were ended by Cardinal Wolsey, the reason being

---

[22] Antonia Fraser, *The Six Wives of Henry VIII* (London: Weidenfeld & Nicolson, 2002) p. 122.

unclear. Perhaps her uncle hoped to marry Butler off to a higher-ranking lady. Whatever the reason, it left Anne unattached. She debuted in court and soon had many young men competing for her hand.

Mary and King Henry

Sometime after Mary returned to England and mysteriously disappears from record, she reemerges as maid-of-honor to Catherine of Aragon, who was the first wife of Henry VIII. Soon after, Mary was wed to an influential and rich courier, William Carey. William was a cousin to the king and was intelligent and had a promising future. The match was advantageous to the Boleyn family, and King Henry apparently approved of the match, too, since he was a guest at the wedding on February 4, 1520.

Apparently, King Henry's attendance at the wedding did nothing to deter him from developing an attraction to Mary. While the notoriety of the affair between King Henry and Mary is well known today, it was very secretive and discreet at the time. The only evidence that exists to credit the liaison is that King Henry applied for a special dispensation from the pope in 1527 to gain permission to marry Anne, and listed in the documents was the mention of Henry's having "illicit intercourse" with Anne's sister.[23] Since this is the only evidence, the date and duration of the affair are complete unknowns; however, most historians speculate that it lasted a period of two to fours years, beginning around 1522. If it was, indeed, a long-standing affair, it most likely would have ended due to Mary's becoming pregnant because in those days pregnant women were to remain discreet during the pregnancy. Many have questioned the fatherhood of her two children, especially her eldest—a daughter—which is still a subject of debate today. Regardless of who the father truly was—whether her husband's or the king's—it would have caused any liaison to cease.

King Henry's Pursuit of Anne

King Henry VIII is known for his weakness for women, much like King Solomon. With six wives how could it be otherwise? Indeed, he did fall victim to his own lust, although he still strove to be reputed as a virtuous king in Christendom. He maintained this view by putting official ends to his previous marriages before making his next one public and by strict discretion as far as his personal affairs were concerned. His greatest struggle seemed to be when his wives were pregnant, and therefore unavailable to him, or when they failed to produce the desired male heir. So naturally, with his previous mistress detached and his current wife

---

[23] H. A. Kelly, *The Matrimonial Trials of Henry VIII* (Eugene, Oregon: Wipf & Stock, 2004), p. 47.

aging and fruitless, it wasn't long before Henry had another young woman in his sights.

Anne Boleyn had become a very popular person in the court of King Henry. She set trends and flourished in the favor of many, especially the king himself.

> *For her excellent gesture and behavior, she did excel all other; in so much that, the king began to grow enamored with her; which was not known to any person, ne so scantly to her own person.*
> *~George Cavendish*[24]

That Cavendish considered Anne to "excel all other" is not a light compliment considering that, if anything, Cavendish was inclined to dislike Anne because of her later animosity toward Cardinal Wolsey. If even her critics considered her so highly, it is easy to see why the king would become "enamored." But he wasn't the only man to notice her.

A young courtier by the name of Henry Percy succeeded in gaining Anne's attention. The problem was, however, that he had been betrothed to someone else since childhood. He and Anne became secretly engaged, which infuriated Percy's father and Cardinal Wolsey, who put an end to the engagement. According to early biographer George Cavendish, King Henry had noticed Anne prior to her infatuation with Percy but had kept his

---

[24] George Cavendish, *The Life of Cardinal Wolsey,* Ebook (Seattle, Wash.: Amazon Digital Services, 2017), p. 50.

affections secret. When her attachment to Percy came to light, the king could no longer hide his feelings for Anne. He revealed himself and his intentions to Cardinal Wolsey, who had the power to put an end to the relationship, since Percy was one of his attendants. When Wolsey approached Percy and told him to forget the infatuation, the young man wept and begged the cardinal to reconsider and allow him to marry Anne. Seeing that further persuasion was needed, Wolsey threatened Percy with disgrace and disinheritance, to which Percy finally yielded.[25] Anne was sent home, still oblivious to King Henry's growing affection, and Percy was married to Lady Mary Talbot, his original intended. According to Cavendish, this was the beginning of the animosity between Anne Boleyn and Cardinal Wolsey.

> *Mistress Anne Boleyn was greatly offended (at his interference with Percy), promising if it ever lay in her power, she would work much displeasure to the Cardinal, as after she did indeed. ~George Cavendish*[26]

After this romance had blown over, Anne returned to court, and King Henry's advances began. However, Anne resisted Henry and refused to become his mistress as her sister had.

---

[25] Ibid., p. 51-54.

[26] Ibid., p. 57.

Perhaps it was because she was aware of her sister's relationship with King Henry and vowed she would not be taken advantage of and then discreetly dumped without any benefit to herself. Or perhaps it was truly because of the piety and religion that had been instilled in her during her time with Queen Claude in France. One can only speculate, since very little documentation exists to give us insight into her thoughts at the time.

Henry courted her for seven years. Eighteen of his love letters to Anne survive, giving us a little bit of insight into his affection for her. He reproaches her for rebuffing him, promises to be true to her, and complains of how painful it is for him to be separated from her.

> *It is absolutely necessary for me to obtain this answer, having been for above a whole year stricken with the dart of love, and not yet sure whether I shall fail of finding a place in your heart and affection..."* ~King Henry's first letter to Anne

We can also glean from these letters that Anne's brother and father were involved in their courtship, bringing Anne to court so she could visit the king.

> *But begging you, my mistress, to tell your father from me, that I desire him to hasten the time appointed by two days, that he may be at court before the old term, or at farthest, on the day prefixed; for otherwise I shall think he will not do*

*the lover's turn, as he said he would, nor answer
my expectation. ~King Henry's thirteenth letter to
Anne*

During this time, the king also raged about the battle to annul his twenty-year marriage to Catherine of Aragon, his brother's widow. King Henry's request for annulment brings out an interesting point with Henry's previous liaison with Mary Boleyn. The affair had to be yet unknown to most people, especially Queen Catherine and her allies, otherwise they would have used the information against the king. Henry claimed that his marriage to Catherine violated his conscience—and the Scriptures according to Leviticus 20:21—because she had first been married to Henry's brother. If they'd known Henry previously had relations with Anne's sister, and yet was attempting to marry Anne, they could have discounted those arguments and declared his marriage with Anne unlawful as well.

When the "sweating sickness" raged in 1528, Anne retreated to her family home. She became very ill, as did Mary's husband. Henry sent his personal physician to treat Anne, and she soon recovered. Her brother-in-law, however, perished of the disease, leaving Mary a widow.

This bout of sickness must have frightened the king because he became even more desperate to marry Anne. The conflict over the annulment of his marriage caused a break from the pope and set the stage for the Protestant Reformation in England.

Anne gained such influence during the period of the king's

courtship of her that ambassadors considered it essential to win her approval if they wanted influence in the English government. She actively encouraged the Reformation movement, often protecting English translators and scholars.

Mary's Second Marriage

Mary had been living at court with her husband, William Carey, until she was widowed in 1528. At that point, Mary was left penniless. Her son, Henry, became the ward of Anne, and King Henry insisted that her father, Thomas Boleyn, take Mary back into his household and provide for her. Why her father was begrudging to do that, history doesn't tell us. Some historians speculate that it was because Mary's reputation as a mistress to King Henry was known to him. Or perhaps she was the lesser sister in the family's eyes, the black sheep because of her past slip-ups. At any rate, letters from Mary later indicate that she was in "bondage" during this time.

A few years later, Mary did the unthinkable. She fell in love with a soldier, William Stafford. Because a soldier was of considerably lower rank, they married in secret and were found out only when Mary's pregnancy became visible. The court, including the newly crowned Queen Anne, was furious. Mary was shunned, and the couple banished from court. Later, Mary appealed her cause to the Master Secretary where she gave this explanation for her "ill-advised" marriage.

> *But one thing, good master secretary, consider,*
> *that he was young, and love overcame reason; and*
> *for my part I saw so much honesty in him, that I*
> *loved him as well as he did me, and was in*
> *bondage, and glad I was to be at liberty: so that,*
> *for my part, I saw that all the world did set so little*
> *by me, and he so much, that I thought I could take*
> *no better way but to take him and to forsake all*
> *other ways, and live a poor, honest life with him.*
> *~Mary Stafford's Letter to Master Secretary*

Her appeals did manage to gain a little compassion from her sister, and she was granted a small pension and the education of her son. Thus, the elder sister lived in poverty with a man she loved, and the younger lived in a lavish but treacherous court as Queen of England. Both came to early deaths.

Anne's Downfall

Anne's demise has become infamous and the subject of much imagination and many retellings. Anne gave birth to a girl, later to become Queen Elizabeth I, but this was her only living child. She suffered two miscarriages, one of which was claimed to be "deformed." The last miscarriage of what was supposed to be a male child on the day of Catherine of Aragon's funeral may have been part of her fall from grace with Henry. He was known to be deeply superstitious and religious and often read into events in his life as signs from God. Was her failure to produce a male heir evidence that he shouldn't have married her? Many historians believe this was a factor. But there were many others as well.

Anne had created many enemies in court after her ascension to the throne, Thomas Cromwell and Cardinal Wolsey among others. She was a spirited person with a temper and a tendency to say too much. Her enemies were waiting for the chance to topple her throne. Cardinal Wolsey and his attendants considered her prideful and disagreeable, as Cavendish mentions:

> *After she knew the king's pleasure and the bottom of his secret stomach, then she began to look very haughty and stout, lacking no manner of jewels or rich apparel, that might be gotten for money. ~ George Cavendish*[27]

Her vitality and banter got her into trouble. Certain remarks, whether in writing or in front of witnesses, brought accusations of adultery, conspiring against the king, and even incest with her brother.

Her relationship with Henry had deteriorated since their marriage, and he was now dabbling with other women--namely, Jane Seymour. Between their heated arguments, jealousy on both sides, the lack of a son, and the marital scars caused by words that shouldn't have been said, Henry's heart had wandered so far from Anne that he would now consider his "darling sweetheart"

---

[27] Cavendish, The Life of Cardinal Wolsey. p. 58.

capable of such crimes.

As to her popularity with the English people, historians can't seem to agree. Some assert that she was terribly unpopular, especially with the Catholic subjects, since most of them defended Catherine of Aragon as the rightful queen. Others assert that she was, indeed, popular as she gave many alms and advocated for the poor.

The allegations had been made, and a trial was set. More than two thousand people were in attendance. While she conducted herself in a stately manner, Anne's fate was sealed with the testimony of her own uncle and her former betrothed. She and her brother—along with the four other men convicted with her—were sentenced to death either by burning at the stake or beheading, whichever the king chose. The king was merciful and ordered that Anne be executed by a particular executioner who was known to be swift with the sword, the "hangman of Calais."

Anne was given communion and spent the night prior to her execution in prayer. As legend would have it, she composed the following poem. Some have attributed it to her brother, but regardless of who wrote it, the mournful, eerie tone fits perfectly with the death of Anne Boleyn.

> *Oh death, rock me asleep, Bring me to quiet rest,*
> *Let pass my weary guiltless ghost; Out of my careful breast.*

Toll on, thou passing bell; Ring out my doleful knell;
Let thy sound my death tell. Death doth draw nigh; There is no remedy.

My pains who can express? Alas, they are so strong;
My dolour will not suffer strength; My life for to prolong.
Toll on, thou passing bell; Ring out my doleful knell;

13 Execution of Anne Boleyn

Let thy sound my death tell. Death doth draw nigh; There is no remedy
Alone in prison strong, I wait my destiny.

Woe worth this cruel hap that I Should taste this misery!
Toll on, thou passing bell; Ring out my doleful knell;
Let thy sound my death tell. Death doth draw nigh; There is no remedy.

Farewell, my pleasures past, Welcome, my present pain!
I feel my torments so increase, That life cannot remain.
Cease now, thou passing bell; Rung is my doleful knell;
For the sound my death doth tell. Death doth draw nigh; There is no remedy.

Anne mounted the scaffold that had been erected for her execution wearing a gray robe and red underskirt. She paused before the crowd of onlookers and begged for permission to address them. She was permitted to speak, although her final words differ in accounts of the day. According to a Spanish chronicler, the Spanish ambassador claimed that she blamed Jane Seymour for her death. With all of the differing accounts, the most commonly accepted one was put down in writing by a member of the English Parliament, Edward Hall.

"Good Christian people, I am come hither to die, according to law, for by the law I am judged to

> *die, and therefore I will speak nothing against it. I come here only to die, and thus to yield myself humbly to the will of the King, my lord. And if in my life, I did ever offend the King's Grace, surely with my death I do now atone. I come hither to accuse no man, nor to speak anything of what whereof I am accused, as I know full well that aught I say in my defense doth not appertain to you. I pray and beseech you all, good friends, to pray for the life of the King, my sovereign lord and yours, who is one of the best princes on the face of the earth, who has always treated me so well that better could not be, wherefore I submit to death with good will, humbly asking pardon of all the world. If any person will meddle with my cause, I require them to judge the best. Thus I take leave of the world, and of you, and I heartily desire you all to pray for me. Oh Lord, have mercy on me! To God I commend my soul!" Anne Boleyn's last words according to Edward Hall*

After this speech, Anne pardoned her executioner, knelt, and readied herself for the blow, taking care to tuck her skirts around her feet. One final act of modesty. So it was on May 19, 1536, Anne Boleyn was beheaded and buried in a plain wooden box beneath the altar of the Church of St. Peter ad Vincula on the Tower grounds; just a couple of days after her brother met the same fate.

Mary Boleyn lived in relative quiet until she died of unknown causes on July 19, 1543, in her early forties, outliving her sister by only seven years.

History Remembers

No English queen has had more impact on the history of the nation than Anne Boleyn. [28]

Both of these women influenced English history during the Reformation era, which in turn influenced the entire world with English translations of Scripture, the break with the Roman Catholic Church, and the possibility of females ruling a nation.

Had Anne not protected the translators, scholars, and those who had been imprisoned for holding Lutheran beliefs, who knows what may have become of the Protestant movement or how long it would have taken for the Scriptures to be available in our own language. She sponsored Tyndale's New Testament and his book *The Obedience of a Christian Man,* encouraged King Henry to read Reformation literature, and encouraged her own ladies in waiting to read the Bible in English. Anne is considered one of the most influential queens of England, a martyr, and the mother of the Protestant movement. Her story is also recorded in

---

[28] Joanna Denny, Anne Boleyn: A New Life of England's Tragic Queen (New York: Da Capo Press, 2007).

Foxe's *Book of Martyrs*, as she was the first English queen to be executed.

Mary's impact is harder to analyze. On the surface, it seems that her three children and influence on King Henry are about all we can account to her. But then again, what influence did she hold over her younger sister and her path in life? If we follow the path of her children, we'll see that they greatly impacted the fate of England and the rule of their cousin, Elizabeth I. It was Mary's children that carried on the Boleyn lineage. So perhaps her influence wasn't so petty after all.

Chapter Six
Mary and Elizabeth Tudor

For our next subject, we return to Tudor England and yet another set of powerful sisters. Queens Mary and Elizabeth, both "firsts" of England.

The two sisters could not have been more opposite. Mary was Roman Catholic, Elizabeth Protestant. Mary executed more than three hundred subjects for their so-called heresy and was nicknamed "Bloody Mary," while Elizabeth was known for her commitment to English peace and prosperity. But both would leave a lasting impact on the world.

Mary's Upbringing

While Mary is usually thought of in a horrible light, if we explore the events leading up to her reign, we can more easily understand her. She was the only child of Henry VIII and Catherine of Aragon to live to adulthood. She was baptized into the Roman Catholic Church shortly after her birth on February 18, 1516. She was well educated and raised primarily by her mother. Her Roman Catholic roots ran deep, as she was the granddaughter of Ferdinand and Isabella, the sponsors of Christopher Columbus' voyage to the New World, and the monarchs who restored Catholicism to Granada, Spain, and defeated the Muslims in those countries.

14 *Young Mary Tudor*

When her father lost all hope of Catherine ever producing a male heir—at least one that would survive—he determined to divorce her. After more than twenty years of marriage, he decided that marrying his brother's widow was incest and, therefore, the marriage was null. He broke ties with the Roman Catholic Church over the dispute and married Anne Boleyn, who then bore Elizabeth I.

If a young girl watched her father break with the religious leaders she deified to marry her mother's maid-of-honor, one wouldn't expect her to be very excited about the union. Needless to say, it didn't make a very warm and fuzzy beginning to Mary and Elizabeth's sisterly relations. If that weren't enough, it wasn't long before King Henry influenced Parliament to deem Mary illegitimate, which shoved her from the line of succession into a poor financial state and later a lady-in-waiting for her younger half-sister.

Elizabeth's Upbringing

Elizabeth Tudor was born to Henry VIII and his second wife, Anne Boleyn, on September 7, 1533. The political uproar surrounding the marriage of her parents and her birth made her a celebrity before she was even born, especially after the court physicians and astrologers predicted that she would be a boy. Obviously, their predictions failed. This was especially a problem for Elizabeth's mother, since King Henry was willing to do almost anything to secure a male heir.

A comment by Venetian ambassador Giovanni Michiel intimates that Elizabeth looked much like her father, and for this reason, he favored her, despite her not being the anticipated prince. He claims that this was the reason why she was exalted above her half-sister and given the title of Princess of Wales. But this security was not to last. Elizabeth's mother, Anne, soon fell from the king's favor and was executed for treason. The rest of Elizabeth's growing up years would be in turmoil.

15 Young Elizabeth Tudor

The relationship between Mary and Elizabeth at this point is very interesting to note. When Edward, their brother, was born to Henry's third wife, Jane Seymour, both sisters were present for his christening in 1537. Young Elizabeth, being four years old at the time, carried the chrisom. The ceremony lasted until after midnight, and when the party was finally dismissed, Mary broke the customary order and took Elizabeth's hand as they left the church. Records from Mary's financial books indicate that she sent many presents to her young half-sister. And letters were exchanged between the two of them.

When Henry VIII married again after Jane Seymour's death,

Elizabeth's fortunes became mostly the same as Mary's. She grew up in her brother Edward's household, watching from a distance as her father pedaled through marriage after marriage. It's no wonder that she never gave in to romantic notions and chose to rule alone. But one instance in particular seems worthy of note.

Henry's fifth wife, Catherine Howard, happened to be a cousin to Anne Boleyn. It is interesting that she fascinated the king almost as much as her cousin had. Perhaps due to their kinship, Catherine showed great kindness to young Elizabeth and took pains to be good to her. But their relationship was not to last. When Elizabeth was only eight years old, Catherine was found guilty of adultery and was beheaded—far too reminiscent of her cousin's fate. Perhaps it was at this time that Elizabeth realized the full truth of what had happened to her mother. How much she was told, and how much she understood cannot be known, since Elizabeth remained oddly silent about the entire situation throughout her life. But it was around this time that young Elizabeth first made her infamous declaration, "I will never marry."

Her father married yet again in 1543, but this time Elizabeth's stepmother, Katherine Parr, took a real interest in the king's children. She felt it her duty to be a mother to them, at least on some level. She had Elizabeth and Edward in her household, oversaw their education and encouraged them to learn the teachings of the Reformed Church. It is perhaps this instruction that grounded both Elizabeth and Edward in the faith that would endure the religious turmoil of the realm.

When she was twelve years of age, Elizabeth did something—unknown to historians yet today—that offended the king. She was banished from court, and it took a year of coaxing and her stepmother's intervention to get her restored to the household.

King Henry VIII's Death

When Henry VIII died in January of 1547, Elizabeth was only fourteen years old. Elizabeth and Edward had been separated by that point, however the lords brought them together before sharing the news about their father's death. It is reported that Edward fell on Elizabeth's shoulder and they both wept so deeply that it touched the heart of everyone present. It seems that despite her father's bad temper and his execution of her mother, Elizabeth somehow retained an admiration and affection for him.

As for Mary, her father's death caused her fortunes to improve. Her young half-brother Edward inherited the throne, but Mary inherited estates and palaces and was named among the heirs should Edward not live to have sons. However, young Edward was also a devout Protestant and wished England to remain so. When he fell ill, he and his advisers appointed an heir that would uphold their religious reforms. But Mary wouldn't be so easily passed over. She rallied support and succeeded in overthrowing Jane Grey and her husband.

Queen Mary's Reign

Just before Mary was to enter London, she met up with Elizabeth in Wanstead so the two could enter the city together. Their greeting was filled with warmth. Mary kissed her sister and took her by the hand as they spoke. It seems that Mary was ready to treat Elizabeth with sisterly kindness, provided that Elizabeth would convert to Catholicism and be reconciled to that church. This would be the marked turning point in their relationship.

16 Queen Mary I

When the two royal sisters entered London, Mary and her advisers noted the almost magical affect that Elizabeth had upon the people. She was too well favored, too much like her father, whom the people all still loved with great loyalty. From that point on, Mary's closest advisers began to undermine Elizabeth's character and influence.

In London, Mary held a requiem mass for her brother, Edward; however, Elizabeth refused to attend that mass, or any other. This displeased Mary, and she declined to see Elizabeth or give her an audience for some time. When at last the two sisters agreed to meet, Elizabeth in great emotion asked Mary if it were her fault that she could not believe the Catholic doctrines. Mary's response was kind, urging that if she went to mass, Elizabeth would come to believe. Elizabeth obeyed; however, it caused great stress for her person, and her health began to suffer. Looking at the historical accounts of Elizabeth's life, it seems that any time she was put under great stress or emotional strain, her health failed her. Something the physicians in 1500s England did not fully understand.

As Mary's agenda of drawing England back to the Roman Catholic Church progressed, tension increased between the two sisters. The constant undermining of Elizabeth's character greatly reduced her station and influence with her sister. She finally recognized that she would do better to remove herself from her sister's court and requested leave to return to her own house.

Mary's advisers prompted her to agree, but to send Elizabeth away with warmth and friendliness so that the young princess would not suspect the spies they would send with her. True to her custom, Mary gave her several gifts. However, Elizabeth was not as naïve as the advisers hoped she would be. She begged Mary not to conclude anything about her or pass judgment upon her, without giving her the chance to speak for herself. Mary consented to her request, and Elizabeth departed. To me, one of the most amazing facts of the Tudor era is that Elizabeth survived the upheaval and became queen after Mary's death. Perhaps their early years and this honest plea had something to do with it. But I believe it was a very cautious approach by Elizabeth and the sovereign hand of God that did it.

As Mary grew older, she realized that unless she married and produced an heir, the throne would go to Elizabeth, and all her work and progress on behalf of Roman Catholicism would be wasted. That simply could not happen. So, despite the public's disapproval, she arranged a marriage to a Catholic prince, Philip II of Spain.

This marriage announcement caused even greater unrest in the country, and a conspiracy was launched to marry Elizabeth to a second cousin of royal blood by the name of Edward Courtenay and put them on the throne. Elizabeth and Courtenay had both objected to the match, but the conspiracy went on without their sanction. While the plot was overthrown by Mary and the Privy Council, Elizabeth was sent to the Tower of London, where she spent two miserable months in confinement.

It was Philip's coming to England that spurred Elizabeth's release from the Tower. He intended to watch her closely and eventually marry her off to one of his own relatives, so he advised Mary to release her to a less obvious location.

On May 19, 1554, Elizabeth was released from the Tower and

transported to Woodstock. The transportation was intended to be secret; however, Elizabeth's popularity made that impossible, and it was evident what a tremendous threat such popularity was to Mary and her agenda. As soon as the princess's barge was spotted, gunners let out a salute. Villages she passed through pealed the church bells; in Ricote, Lord Williams of Tame held a banquet in her honor attended by the neighboring gentry. But once they reached Woodstock, Elizabeth's existence was still one of imprisonment. Still, throughout this time of trial and turmoil, Elizabeth turned to her faith for comfort. She wrote on the flyleaf of her edition of St. Paul's Epistles:

> *August. I walk many times into the pleasant fields of the Holy Scriptures, where I pluck up the goodlisome herbs of sentences by pruning, eat them by reading, chew them by musing, and lay them up at length in the high seat of memorie, by gathering them together, that so, having tasted their sweetness, I may the less perceive the bitterness of this miserable life.*[29]

On July 25, 1554, Queen Mary was wed to Prince Philip of Spain. By this time, the old kindness and gentle manner toward her sister seems to have dissolved altogether. The ceremony was performed without so much as a message to her younger half-

---

[29] Antonia Fraser, ed., *Agnes Strickland's Lives of the Queens of England* (London: Continuum International Publishing Group, 2011) p. 113.

sister, much less her attendance or participation. And Mary's note to the lord in charge of Elizabeth's welfare reveals how low her opinion and trust of her sister had fallen. She believed that the conspirators would not have dared their scheme "unless they had knowledge of her [Elizabeth's] favor...than is yet confessed by her."

Unfortunately, Mary's marriage was unsuccessful and unhappy. Apparently, her husband wearied of her quickly and left England to return to Spain, not returning to see her very often. After several miscarriages and false pregnancies, Mary succumbed to an illness that is believed to have been uterine cancer or ovarian cysts. She died on November 17, 1558, only four years after her marriage to Philip, and was buried in Westminster Abbey.

Upon Mary's death, her husband, Prince Philip, wrote in a letter to his sister the princess of Portugal, "I felt a reasonable regret for her death." Such was the intense romance of their marriage.

When the lords of the Privy Council reached Elizabeth with the news, she was walking the grounds at Woodstock. Upon receiving their greeting, she fell to her knees and quoted in Latin the words of the 118th Psalm:

> *This is the LORD's doing; it is marvellous in our eyes.*

For this reason, these words in Latin are inscribed on the British coins honoring Queen Elizabeth I.

The Reign of Queen Elizabeth I

When Elizabeth I ascended to the throne at twenty-five years of age, she had quite a mess on her hands. She was only the third queen to rule England, and the previous two, her half-sister, Mary, and her cousin Lady Jane Grey, had not painted a promising picture. I can only imagine her stress and anxiety as she wondered whether she would end up buried at the Tower of London near the decapitated body of her mother. However, the gifts and skills she both learned and inherited proved invaluable to her as she began her reign, and the people were immediately enamored of her.

> *Her father's ability and his physical magnetism, infused with something of her mother's fascination, had distilled themselves into a personal magic that was admitted even by those who distrusted and disliked her.*[30]

For a young woman of only twenty-five, she had no easy task before her. The country was weak, bankrupt, and torn by religious tension. Her supporters and councilors believed the only way she would succeed would be to quickly find a husband to help her rule. She disagreed, which would become a source of contention between herself and the Privy Council.

Even before her official coronation, Elizabeth held meetings

---

[30] Elizabeth Jenkins, *Elizabeth the Great* (New Haven, Conn.: Phoenix Press, 2000).

with the Council to address the urgent matters of the nation. She was determined to take a balanced approach to religion, unlike her siblings had done before her, and heal the rift that had been pushed nearly to civil war.

17 *Queen Elizabeth I*

"There is only one Christ Jesus and one faith: the rest is a dispute about trifles." ~Queen Elizabeth I

Protestants have criticized Queen Elizabeth I for compromising the Reformed doctrines and not taking a stronger stand against the Catholics, especially coming out of Mary's persecutions. But what we see from Elizabeth is an appreciation for her position as ruler of a diverse people. She did not believe it was her right to tell the people what to believe—as Mary and even Edward had believed. Instead, she saw a kingdom that was close to half Catholic and half Reformed. Her responsibility was to create a country in which both religions were free to exercise their faith and "live peaceably" as the Scriptures point out. Her level-headed approach and management of affairs was the salvation of England.

The Roman Catholic Church, however, did not find her policies acceptable either. While the largest portion of Catholics in England seemed content, Pope Pius V issued a papal bull excommunicating Queen Elizabeth as "the pretended Queen of England" and declaring her an enemy of the church. While the papal declaration asserted that she had with "strong hand inhibited the exercise of the true Religion" and "that the persecution of the faithful, and affliction for Religion, groweth every day heavier and heavier, through the Instigation and Means of the said Elizabeth" the truth was that the Roman Catholic authorities needed to force the English Catholics into action one way or another.[31] Her leniency had made them lackadaisical, which didn't suit the purposes of the pope. In reality, the pope's declaration made things worse for the Catholics in England, because now they were forced to choose between loyalty to their country and loyalty to their religion, which made them enemies of one or the other. It also caused the English government to make stricter laws in order to protect the queen. A great number of

---

[31] 1570 Damnation and Excommunication of Elizabeth Queen of England by Pope Pius V

Catholics converted to Protestantism. However, Elizabeth did the best she could to maintain the goal of making the realm suitable to both Catholic and Protestant religions, which caused criticism from every side.

One of Elizabeth's pet projects was the Royal Navy. Naval expansion had been started by Mary, but had been largely neglected by previous monarchs. Elizabeth saw the navy as a vital element of a safe and peaceable England. She undertook a shipbuilding program and enacted pay raises for men in the naval occupation. William Camden, known as Elizabeth's first biographer, records the following comments on her shipbuilding program.

> *She provided her fleet of all manner of tackling and munition, the best-appointed navy that ever Britain saw. For the defense thereof, she erected a castle upon the bank of Medway near Upmore, and increased the sailors and mariners pay; insomuch as she was worthily named by the Foreigners, The Restorer of the Glory of Shipping and The Queen of the North Sea.*[32]

Despite Queen Elizabeth's early and vehement declaration that she would never marry, much of her reign was spent arguing

---

[32] William Camden, *The History of the Most Renowned and Victorious Prince Elizabeth, Late Queen of England,* Classics of British Historical Literature (Chicago: Univ. of Chicago Press, 1970).

with her Privy Council about arranging a marriage and bearing a son to take the throne upon her death. She was involved in many courtships and potential alliances throughout the years, but although she came close, she never did finalize a marriage contract. However, it was obvious that the queen enjoyed the attention and excitement of courtship, which must be where all of the rumors and speculation as to why she never tied the knot come from.

The end of Elizabeth's reign was not so glorious. Public affection for her began to wane as costs of war and poor harvests depleted the economy. In 1603, following the deaths of several close friends, Queen Elizabeth I fell into a severe depression. It is this melancholy that accounts for her death more than the illness that she suffered.

History Remembers

Despite Queen Mary's short reign and premature death, she did leave a lasting impact on the Western world. She was the first queen to succeed in claiming the English throne. Her reign was a step toward the feminist movement. In fact, John Knox's pamphlet *First Blast of the Trumpet Against the Monstrous Regiment of Women* (quite a mouthful of a title, hmm?) was directed mainly at her and her cousin, Mary Queen of Scots. While most of Mary's policies failed, and she left her country in a bad situation, many of Elizabeth's successes began with Mary's naval expansion, fiscal reform, and exploration of colonies being the notable ones. She also further pressed the Catholic vs. Protestant conflict, which in turn propelled the Reformation and the translation of Scriptures into English.

18 *British Coin Depicting Elizabeth*

As for Elizabeth, she is to this day considered one of the greatest monarchs in English history. The period of her reign is considered the "Golden Age" for many reasons. Her influence on the Reformation and the prosperity of England are monumental. At that time, the world was largely controlled by Roman Catholic countries. However, when Queen Elizabeth and her new navy defeated the Spanish Armada, Protestant foreign missions became a possibility. In fact, some historians credit Elizabeth with the Protestant nature of the United States.

> *Had the Spanish Armada not been defeated,*
> *Protestantism could have been extinguished in*
> *England and Holland. And then the whole future of*
> *North America would have been far different with*

Catholicism dominating instead of the Protestant Pilgrims.[33]

It was Elizabeth who repaired the credit of the English government, built up the navy, increased the literacy and cultural achievements in the country and encouraged science. She also established "Poor Laws," which provided the framework to aid those in need. She extinguished rebellions and conspiracies, and throughout her reign, with all her faults, she maintained the love and adoration of her subjects. She considered England her husband and remained faithful to him until her death.

In the end, Elizabeth was buried next to her sister, Mary, in Westminster Abbey. Despite their differences and contrasts, they share the same epitaph, which translated from Latin reads, *"Consorts in realm and tomb, here we sleep, Elizabeth and Mary, sisters, in hope of resurrection."*

---

[33] Philip Hammond, "The Spanish Armada," ReformationSA.org, www.reformationsa.org.

Chapter Seven
Sarah and Angelina Grimke

In the heartland of southern plantations, born during the height of the antebellum era, were two women with strong convictions and independent thinking. Although thirteen years apart, sisters Sarah and Angelina Grimké were very close and became legends during their own lifetimes.

These sisters banded together in what is probably the closest bond out of all the sisters that we have studied, and together they changed the world for the good and delivered many from the oppressor.

The Grimké Heritage

Sarah was the sixth child born into the home of a wealthy South Carolina family on November 26, 1792. Her father was a prominent Charleston judge and a slaveholder who had served as a colonel during the Revolutionary War. The Grimké family was a centerpiece in Charleston society, holding great influence in the community. They were faithful Episcopalians and attended church regularly. The family name of Grimké carried weight, which would later aid as well as complicate things for Sarah and her sister.

As Sarah grew, her parents soon realized they had a special child on their hands. Her intellect was sharp, her reasoning keen, and her sense of justice acute. Her brother Thomas, six years her senior, was her dearest companion, and they often studied and conversed together on a great many subjects. Sarah's interest in education and learning became a point of contention, as she wanted to pursue subjects such as law and Latin, which were considered to be masculine subjects at the time. Sarah had begun to learn Latin in private and was forbidden to continue when her father discovered it. Even her brother discouraged her learning on masculine topics. However, her father did give Sarah special attention when it came to academics. Her mental capabilities excited his fatherly pride, and he is said to have remarked that if she had been born a man, she would have made the best jurist in the land.[34]

John Grimké was a strict disciplinarian who believed his children should learn hard work. As a result, he would often send them out to labor among the slaves in the cotton and corn fields. Although we don't know the exact instances, it must have been here that Sarah, as well as her younger sister, Angelina, saw something at a young age that made a very deep impression on them. It caused them to fiercely oppose slavery, despite the contrary opinions of the rest of their family and friends. In speaking of her experiences in the fields working alongside slaves, Sarah would say:

---

[34] Catherine H. Birney, The Grimké Sisters Sarah and Angelina Grimké: The First American Women Advocates of Abolition and Woman's Rights (Los Angeles: HardPress Publishing, 2006).

Perhaps I am indebted partially to this for my life-long detestation of slavery, as it brought me in close contact with these unpaid toilers. ~from the diaries of Sarah Grimké

According to biographer Catherine H Birney, the scenes Sarah witnessed affected her so deeply that she was "frequently found in some retired spot weeping after one of the slaves had been punished."[35]

The Formation of a Lifelong Bond

When Sarah was about thirteen years old, she would experience two great changes in her way of life. First, Thomas was sent off to college, leaving her without her studying companion. Without him, she was lonely and inconsolable. A couple of weeks after his departure, her baby sister was born, the fourteenth and last child of her parents. Sarah adopted this sister as her own darling, the beginning of a bond that would last a lifetime and change the world as they knew it.

Angelina was born February 20, 1805, the caboose to her parent's large family train. She was a beautiful child with ringlets of auburn hair, clear blue eyes, and a cheerful disposition. Much like her elder sister, Angelina inherited a keen intellect and love of learning. Sarah begged her parents to allow her to be named as

---

[35] Ibid.

Angelina's godmother. At first, her parents refused, not believing a child the age of thirteen had any real understanding of what that meant. When the fancy didn't pass and Sarah continued to plead, they at last gave in. Sarah was named Angelina's godmother at her christening, a responsibility she took very seriously.

19 Sarah Grimké

As Sarah entered the social scene around age sixteen, she was drawn into the fashionable lifestyle. While she flitted about from party to party, gathering to gathering, and became increasingly popular, something inside of her was not satisfied. She knew there had to be something more, something deeper than this frivolous and shallow society of appearances. Her soul was thirsting, but the traditional services at the Episcopalian church did nothing to quench it.

The Start of Something Deeper

One night, Sarah attended a meeting at a Presbyterian church where a man by the name of Reverend Henry Kolloch was speaking. His sermon moved Sarah greatly; however, as soon as she was back under the influence of her fashionable friends, that spark died out. For another year, she was distracted from her spiritual well-being and occupied with social activities. Reverend Kolloch came to town again, and this time Sarah was doubly affected; however, she still held back in reserve. How could she give up the pleasures her family's name had granted her? She felt she should, but simply couldn't.

It was then that Sarah went on a trip to the country with her friends. As Providence would have it, Reverend Kolloch just so happened to meet her there. As they spoke, the reverend took an interest in the young woman and her spiritual welfare. While his conversations excited her conscience and her desire to change, she endeavored to do so by her own works and merits. She became very active in doing charitable works, but her soul remained in torment.

> *I, therefore, set earnestly to work to do good according to my capacity. I fed the hungry and clothed the naked, I visited the sick and afflicted,*

and vainly hoped these outside works would purify a heart defiled with the pride of life, still the seat of carnal propensities and evil passions; but here, too, I failed. I went mourning on my way under the curse of a broken law; and, though I often watered my couch with my tears, and pleaded with my Maker, yet I knew nothing of the sanctifying influence of his holy spirit, and, not finding that happiness in religion I anticipated, I, by degrees, through the persuasions of companions and the inclination of my depraved heart, began to go a little more into society, and to resume my former style of dressing, though in comparative moderation. ~from the diaries of Sarah Grimké

While the reverend did visit her again, his rebukes only made Sarah more miserable. She immersed herself in entertainments in an effort to drown out the cry of her soul. This created what Sarah considered a downward spiral until the "merciful interposition of Providence" changed her course.

The Intervention of Providence

*I know not where I might have been landed, had
not the merciful interposition of Providence
stopped my progress.*[36]

Sarah's father fell ill and was advised to take a trip to the north in hopes that a doctor in Philadelphia could help him. This trip would be one of the most important events in Sarah's life. While in the north, Sarah attended a Methodist assembly. The preaching there affected her greatly, and she was aroused from the stupor that her entertainment and fashionable lifestyle had thrown her into. No longer apathetic to religion, she was influenced by some acquaintances of the Quaker faith in Philadelphia. While she did not fully agree with them at first, she began to consider more doctrinal themes.

The trip did not heal her father's health, however, and after his death, Sarah returned home to Charleston. Apparently, the Quaker influence was strong, because her siblings began to tease her in that regard. Her brother jokingly gifted her with a book on the Quaker faith, which she read. The writing raised questions in her mind, and she began corresponding with her friends in Philadelphia. Some months later, she converted wholly to Quakerism, beginning by removing lace, ribbons, and adornments from her fashionable attire.

---

[36] Ibid.

Sarah's mind now settled on spiritual things and the good of others, and her detestation of slavery festered. Soon, her opinions made life in a slavery-driven community unbearable, and Sarah moved to a Quaker settlement in Pennsylvania in May 1821.

Angelina's Spiritual Journey

Angelina grew up—much like her older sister—to be a cheery, fashionable, and popular member of society. Her beauty and wit made her the subject of admiration for many. She was more inspiring than her sister, more self-assured, and arguably more brilliant than Sarah. These qualities made her life in Charleston a happy one. It seems that Angelina at first consented to the practice of slavery, taking passages from the Bible as consent to own them. That, of course, would change.

While Angelina's spiritual path follows many of the same steps as her elder sister's, the way she experienced them was quite in contrast. Again, I refer to a comment by historian and biographer Catherine H. Birney, who describes the difference:

> *In her humility, and in her strong reliance on the "inner light," Sarah refused to trust her own judgment, even in the merest trifles, such as the lending of a book to a friend, postponing the writing of a letter, or sweeping a room to-day, when it might be better to defer it until to-morrow.*

Angelina, on the other hand, was wonderfully well satisfied with her own power of distinguishing right from wrong; this power being, she believed, the gift of the Spirit to her. She sought her object, dreading no consequences, and if disaster followed she comforted herself with the feeling that she had acted according to her best light. She was a faithful disciple of every cause she espoused and scrupulously exact in obeying even its implied provisions. In this, there was no hesitancy. [37]

20 Angelina Grimke

---

[37] Ibid., chapter 4.

Where Sarah struggled in giving up her self-will, Angelina relinquished it as a glad offering. Where Sarah felt burdened, Angelina felt joy and peace. Such were the great differences in their temperament and relationship with the Creator.

Much to her mother's dismay, Angelina also began attending a Presbyterian church. She participated in the services, taught Sunday school, joined in many of the charitable works, and was an integral part of their assembly. However, Angelina soon found a lack in her church-going ways. As she studied, read and drew closer to the Lord, she felt strangely compelled to leave the Presbyterian church and instead fellowship with the Quakers. She, too, became convicted about her manner of dress and began to change it to be more plain and modest.

Angelina's outspoken nature caused her family problems when she began to feel convicted about her family's lavish lifestyle. If Christians were to be humble servants of God, discreet and unselfish, then the Grimké household was a poor example. This opinion caused many arguments between Angelina and her family, especially her mother.

The main strength and encouragement to Angelina at this time were the letters she received from Sarah. Angelina said in a letter to Sarah:

> *Thou art, dearest, my best beloved, and often does my heart expand with gratitude to the Giver of all good for the gift of such a friend, who has been the helper of my joy and the lifter up of my hands*

when they were ready to hang down in hopeless despair.[38]

During this time, Angelina's views on slavery also changed. It was due in part to her spiritual enlightenment, in part to instances she witnessed in Charleston, and also in part to Sarah's influence. Sarah sent her anti-slavery literature, and Angelina could contrast the words with what she saw day to day being inflicted upon the slaves all around her. Her heart became so burdened for the slaves that her letters and diaries emit a real suffering, an acute pain as if she were living as a slave herself and suffering every blow she chanced to witness.

In 1829, Angelina followed her sister to Pennsylvania. Despite their disagreements, her parting with her mother was warm. Angelina's mother embraced her, saying through her tears, "Joseph is not, and Simeon is not, and ye will take Benjamin away also!" This loving parting must have been a great comfort to Angelina in later years, for this would be the last time she would see her mother.

Angelina settled in as a member of the Quaker community in Philadelphia. While she did not wholly agree with them—as Sarah did—she joined as an official member of their Society, which seems to have been out of respect for her sister.

It is interesting to note that Sarah went through several years in the Quaker community with a feeling of despair. She felt called

---

[38] Ibid., chapter 6

to speak as a minister during their meetings, which was acceptable in the Society at that time. However, whenever she did so, she met with such disapproval from the elders that it caused her great distress. For several years she was unfulfilled and unhappy. This work does not allow ample space for me to go into detail, but if not for Angelina's lead, Sarah may have remained in that unhappy state for the rest of her life.

An Unexpected Occupation

After their move to Pennsylvania, Angelina's public career began accidentally. In 1835, the renowned abolitionist William Lloyd Garrison published an appeal in Boston begging the people to leave off violence. Anti-Abolition demonstrations resulted in mobs of angry people and violence was becoming frequent, especially in New York, Pennsylvania, and South Carolina. For some reason, Angelina felt compelled to send the man a personal letter of encouragement. Garrison ended up publishing the letter in an issue of *The Liberator*, much to the embarrassment of Angelina and the shock of her Quaker neighbors. This was the start of her and her sister's public career.

While Angelina was scolded by her Quaker friends, she felt the Lord compelled her to act on behalf of the slave. After much prayer, she emerged with the inspiration to write a pamphlet to the southern Christian woman on the subject of slavery. About the time she began writing this pamphlet, a man from the Anti-Slavery Society in New York wrote to her requesting that she

12 Sisters Who Changed History

come and speak to the women of the society. Theodore Weld, the future husband of Angelina, records her reaction to the invitation in his tribute to her.

> *It was stated at the funeral that the Executive Committee of the American Anti-slavery Society wrote to -Miss Grimke, inviting her to visit New York City, and hold meetings in private parlors, with Christian women, on the subject of slavery. Upon reading their letter, she handed it to her sister Sarah, saying : "I feel this to be God's call. I cannot decline it."[39]*

The Quaker leaders greatly opposed this notion, but Angelina believed it was part of God's calling on her life.

She finished the pamphlet and sent it off to the Anti-Slavery Society, who published the work with great enthusiasm. The amount of disapproval, both in the north and the south, was mind blowing. The Quakers scolded and threatened to disown Angelina, while her contemporaries in South Carolina berated her and threatened to arrest or harm her if she returned to visit her family.

Theodore Weld, Angelina's future husband, gave this account of the reception of her pamphlet:

---

[39] Theodore Weld, *In Memory: Angelina Grimké Weld* (London: Forgotten Books, 2018).

> *When it came out, a large number of copies were sent by mail to South Carolina. Most of them were publicly burned by postmasters. Not long after this, the city authorities of Charleston learned that Miss Grimké was intending to visit her mother and sisters, and pass the winter with them. Thereupon the mayor called upon Mrs. Grimké and desired her to inform her daughter that the police had been instructed to prevent her landing while the steamer remained in port, and to see to it that she should not communicate, by letter or otherwise, with any persons in the city; and, further, that if she should elude their vigilance and go on shore, she would be arrested and imprisoned until the return of the vessel. Her Charleston friends at once conveyed to her the message of the mayor, and added that the people of Charleston were so incensed against her, that if she should go there despite the mayor's threat of pains and penalties, she could not escape personal violence at the hands of the mob.[40]*

Taking the issue to prayer, Angelina sought the Lord's correction or courage. Had she done wrong in publishing the pamphlet? Comparing her attitude to the Scriptures, Angelina

---

[40] Ibid., p. 58.

stood firm, knowing in her heart that the Bible supported her stand against slavery and that her God-given position had enabled her to speak as others could not.

Angelina accepted the invitation to become a speaker for the Anti-Slavery Society and discovered her gift. She soon became known as the most powerful and stirring female orator for the abolitionist cause.

A Sisterly Alliance – The Dynamic Dou

Where was Sarah in all this commotion? Thomas, Sarah's beloved companion and brother, had died of cholera, and this was a great blow to her. While she endeavored to bear it as God's will, it further depressed her spirits.

Since Angelina had moved to Shrewsbury, Pennsylvania, prior to writing the infamous letter to Garrison, she had corresponded with Sarah via letters. Sarah had joined the Quaker's side in the matter, and rebuked Angelina by saying that she should not have sent it or had her name published in such a manner. However, a couple of days after the letter came out, Sarah was publicly degraded by the presiding elder of her community during one of her ministering talks. She had stood up to share a few words of encouragement, as was a custom with the Quakers, and yet the elder interrupted her and made her sit down without giving any apparent reason. This was the surfacing of an underlying tension that had been brooding between Sarah and the elders for some time. She was their target of criticism and harshness, yet she had no understanding as to what she had done wrong—if anything—and what would cause them to direct such animosity toward her. This event greatly wounded her trust in the Quaker Society and their leaders.

When Angelina was considering writing *An Appeal to the Christian Women of the South,* she had written to Sarah to get her thoughts. Sarah wrote back sympathetically, telling her that if she felt called by God to do it, she would support her, although Sarah herself did not believe it to be wise. Angelina was very grateful for her sister's support. Sarah had been a second mother to her, and her approval was of immeasurable comfort.

After the public humiliation, Sarah moved for a short time to Burlington, Pennsylvania. In August of 1836, the two sisters were reunited when Sarah accepted the invitation to join Angelina in Shrewsbury. It appears that Sarah's mind, now being liberated from the oppression of the elders in Philadelphia, had come to agree very much with Angelina's views. Unfortunately, we know very little about Sarah's thoughts at this time, since she left off her journal keeping for a period.

When Angelina spoke to Sarah about her call to New York in order to aid the Anti-Slavery Society, Sarah's response must have surprised but delighted her. In her biography, Catherine H. Birney records the exchange.

> *If thou indeed feelest thus, and I cannot doubt it, then my mind too is made up. Where thou goest, I will go; thy God shall be my God, thy people my*

people. What thou doest, I will, to my utmost, aid thee in doing. We have wept and prayed together, we will go and work together." And thus fully united, heart and soul and mind, they departed for New York.[41]

The dynamic duo began by speaking in parlors to small groups of women, but soon they were addressing large crowds of females and had created another branch of the society especially for women. It wasn't long before they began touring around New York, New Jersey, and the rest of New England, speaking to audiences about what they had witnessed of slavery while growing up and the need for abolition. They kept up an amazing schedule, sometimes speaking as many as six times per week.

Besides their speaking tours, the sisters wrote books, abolitionist tracts, and pamphlets. Angelina became the first woman in America to address a body of legislators. Sarah may not have dazzled audiences with her speech as Angelina did, but she was mighty with the pen.

Angelina's Marriage

Through the American Anti-Slavery Society, Angelina became acquainted with the abolitionist and speaker Theodore Weld in October of 1836. From her diaries, it is clear that she was

---

[41] Birney, *The Grimke Sisters*, chap. 11.

very impressed with him from the first time she met him. Theodore became an avid supporter of the two sisters, encouraging them when most of the people around them disapproved of their methods and ideas. He even supported Angelina's opinions on women's rights. They enjoyed a friendship and close ties as coworkers in the abolitionist cause for about two years before they married. The proposal apparently came about through an argument. Weld had written to Angelina, asserting that women's rights should not be her focus until after the slaves were freed. To this, Angelina replied in pain and anger: "Can you not stand side-by-side with us?" She went on to admit that she hadn't realized how much he disliked her. In his heated reply to that remark, Weld called her a youth full of pride and anger, then in letters twice the size of the rest he wrote, "I have loved you since the first moment I met you."[42]

Their marriage ceremony was very untraditional. Angelina did not believe in being married by a clergyman, so instead the couple opted for twelve witnesses. One of those witnesses was an African American minister who led prayer during the service. The couple also did not use traditional vows but spoke from the heart. Weld denounced the "unrighteous power" that the American culture gave a husband over his wife and required only the influence that love could wield over a person. It seems the two were wonderfully suited, and they were very happy together.

---

[42] Historian Carol Birkin on **"The Abolitionists," Part 1 of** *The American Experience,* PBS (January 8, 2012).

Because of her marriage, however, both sisters were expelled from the Quaker Society. Weld explains:

> *So, also, the rule that any one who should marry out of the Society should, unless penitent, be disowned. Consequently, when Angelina thus married, she was disowned, as was Sarah for sanctioning the marriage by her presence.*[43]

Theodore, Angelina, and Sarah continued to work toward racial equality together. Their great efforts would pay off.

History Remembers

Angelina's dynamic speaking career came to an abrupt end two days after her wedding. Tensions were high at the anti-slavery convention on May 16, 1838. Angry crowds in Philadelphia turned violent as she stood in the convention hall and gave her last stirring speech. "I have seen it! I know it has horrors that can never be described." The next morning, the mob burned and destroyed the building, offices and everything inside. Her husband described the results:

> *Early in her married life, she was twice severely injured. These injuries, though wholly unlike, were in their effect a unit, one causing, the*

---

[43] Weld, In Memory: Angelina Grimke Weld.

other intensifying a life-long weakness. Together they shattered incurably her nervous system. The one was wholly internal: the other caused a deep wound which never healed. Such was the effect upon her, that even after she was forced to avoid exciting scenes and topics, especially slavery, its effects upon slave and master, also the wrongs of woman as wrought out in her legal, ecclesiastical, educational, and political disabilities, by which through all time she had been fettered, shriveled, and palsied. Add to these the horrible inflictions upon children by passionate parents and teachers. Once hearing the frantic screams of a whipped child, alternated with outbursts of parental rage, prostrated her for an entire day, and filled with moanings the fitful dreams of a half-sleepless night. These severe injuries, with the morbid ailments resulting, unbraced for life her nervous system. All special mental anxiety and distress produced thenceforward such faintness and sense of sinking that from the first she would say : " My mission is over. He who gave it has taken it." She never afterward spoke in public.[44]

However, she, her husband and her sister continued to write

---

[44] Ibid.

and educate. Angelina raised three children, ran two schools, and continued to advocate for abolition, women's rights, and other humanitarian causes. The sisters supported Abraham Lincoln during the Civil War and lived to see the end of slavery before their deaths.

Sarah died in December of 1873 at the ripe old age of eighty-one. Angelina's health declined after a series of strokes had left her paralyzed, and she died in October 1879.

The views of these two sisters were radical, even among their own ranks of abolitionists. They were pioneers in the belief that not only was slavery wrong but also that the African Americans should be treated the same as whites. They were also proponents of women's suffrage, which was practically unknown during those days. They were threatened, exiled, railed against, and hailed as heroes by various groups. Yet today they leave a strong legacy of social reform and anti-racism. They were the first to hold an assembly of women, not Quakers, in a public place in America, while Angelina was the first woman to address a body of legislators. Because of their monumental influence, the Grimké sisters were inducted into the National Women's Hall of Fame.

Chapter Eight
Conclusion

In this study of sisters who changed history, we have seen women born into poor families, military families, even royal families. But their births are not what made history remember them. Had queens Mary I and Elizabeth I died shortly after birth, as so many of their siblings had, they would not be names mentioned in every world history book.

We've studied sisters who teamed up together, had close relationships, and suffered the same fate; while others fought against each other, held bitterness and hatred for each other, and even threatened each other's lives.

While each of these sisters were extraordinary in their own right, they were also regular people (with the exception of Athena and Artemis) who had quirks, faults, and failures. They had no defining talents that made them change the world; they had only what Providence had provided for them.

So what made these women different? What gave them the capacity to change the world?

They discovered their calling and pursued it with purpose.

For Rachel and Leah, their calling was to be a wife to Jacob and a mother to his children. They pursued that calling with purpose and became the mothers of princes and nations. For the Tru'ng sisters, their calling was to make a stand against oppression of the enemy in their country. Their pursuit brought victory, inspiration, and eventually freedom to their people. Mary and Anne Boleyn were called to influence kings, and they did so, bringing about the dawn of the Reformation. Mary and Elizabeth had the calling to restore spiritual and financial prosperity to England, and each did so in very different—almost opposite—ways. Sarah and Angelina Grimké had a calling to free the oppressed slaves in their nation, and they pursued it with passion never before seen in their time by their sex. These women changed history and inspired multitudes because they found something worth fighting for and took action.

But this study is not yet over. As you think about the women you've read about in this book, it is now time for you to study your own heart. Regardless of the circumstance of your birth or your family's status or your inborn talents and abilities, there is a purpose for your life. Regardless of what your current relationship with your siblings may be or what faults and failures you may harbor, Providence has given you the capacity to make a difference.

What is the calling in your life? To give life to a family? To raise warriors of truth? To speak courage and faith in a world of suicide? To testify to something greater than yourself?

What do you see is worth fighting for? Marriage? Life of the innocent? Truth?

What are you going to do about it? How can you change the world, as we know it, for the better? In a world filled with injustice, cruelty, and evil, what impression will you leave when God calls you home?

The story of sisters who changed history will not be complete until you can answer these questions for yourself. I challenge you to consider this prayerfully. Ignore the fear, open the door to every room in your heart, and ask the Lord to show you what His purpose is for your life. It may be that the darkest, most painful places are the ones He wants to use, but through that process the blessed peace of healing will fill those empty spaces.

Discover your God-given calling, pray for the strength and courage to pursue it, then start changing your world. Even if it's one kind word at a time.

Thank you for Reading

Thank you so much for joining me for 12 Sisters Who Changed History! If you enjoyed this book, please consider leaving a review, sharing with your friends on social media, or requesting it at your local library.

If we haven't met, I'd love to make your acquaintance! I love meeting and talking to other readers and lovers of history. You can find me on my website, **http://www.Amberschamel.com**, or at any of the following:

Sign up for our Newsletter and get a Short Story FREE! subscribe to our newsletter here.

Blogs - **http://stitchesthrutime.blogspot.com/**
      http://www.hhhistory.com/
      http://amberschamel.blogspot.com/

Facebook - **https://www.facebook.com/AuthorAmberSchamel**
Twitter - @AmberSchamel **https://twitter.com/AmberSchamel**
Pinterest - **http://pinterest.com/AmberDSchamel/**
Goodreads - **https://www.goodreads.com/author/show/7073165.Amber_Schamel**

Further Reading

If you would like to learn more about these fascinating characters, below is a list of books I discovered during my research.

- *The Holy Bible* (Genesis 29-32 & Acts 19)
- Ancient History Encyclopedia- *Athena* and also *Artemis* both by Mark Cartwright
- The Bible Commentary by Matthew Henry (Genesis 29-32)
- *Book of the Later Han* by Fan Ye
- The Anne Boleyn Files website: **https://www.theanneboleynfiles.com/**
- *The Life of Cardinal Wolsey* by George Cavindish
- *Mary Boleyn: The Mistress of Kings* by Alison Weir
- *Love Letters of Henry VIII to Anne Boleyn* Compiled by J.W. Luce (1906)
- *Anne Boleyn: The Biography* by University Press
- *Elizabeth the Great* by Elizabeth Jenkins
- *The History of the Most Renowned and Victorious Princess Elizabeth, Late Queen of England: Containing all the Most Important and Remarkable Passages of State, Both at Home, and Abroad (so far as they were linked with English affairs) During Her Long and Prosperous Reign* by William Camden
- Reformation SA Website: www.reformationsa.org

- *The Defamation and Excommunication of Elizabeth Queen of England* by Pope Pius V (1570)
- *The Grimke Sisters: Sarah & Angelina Grimke the first American women advocates of abolition and women's rights* by Catherine H. Birney
- *An Appeal to the Christian Women of the South* by Angelina Emily Grimke
- *In Memory: Angelina Grimke Weld* by Theodore Dwight Wells

Other Books by Amber Schamel

Biblical Fiction

The Swaddling Clothes

Through the ages, men have told many stories about Mary, Joseph, and the birth of the Messiah. Stories of shepherds and sheep, kings, angels, and stables. But one story no one has ever told. One story hidden in the fabric of time. The story of The Swaddling Clothes.

Days of Messiah Series

Book One - The Healer's Touch: Aaliyah's last chance at winning her husband's love is destroyed when she is banished from her home as an 'unclean' sinner, exiled to the leper colony. When a chance at being cured comes in the form of a rumor, she must risk her life to appear in public, or die a leper.

Book Two – The Messiah's Sign: After banishing his unfaithful wife to a leper colony, Tyrus struggles to raise and protect their son. But when Malon begins following the teacher from Nazareth, what remains of their business and reputation is at stake. Saving his son from a sinister outlaw could cost him everything, but the beguiling lies of a false messiah may cost him more.

Book Three – The Master's Calling: Malon believes his life calling is to become a disciple of the Messiah and help free Israel from bondage. When at last his family consents to let him go, Malon arrives in Jerusalem only to discover that he is too late. The man he thought to be the Messiah has been crucified, and Barabbas—his greatest enemy—has been set free.

All Amber's titles are available on Amazon or at www.Amberschamel.com.

Award-Winning Historical Fiction

Dawn of Liberty – 2017 Christian Indie Award Winner

Liberty comes with a price. Can a fledgling nation bear the cost?

British forces advance upon a struggling colonial army. The time of decision has come. Declare independence or give up the fight. The weight of a nation rests on Samuel Adams' shoulders as he joins the delegates of the Second Continental Congress. Can he raise the cause of Liberty above the fear of the King's wrath in the hearts of his countrymen?

Three riveting short stories follow Samuel Adams as he struggles through the events surrounding the Declaration of Independence and evokes the Dawn of Liberty.

Solve by Christmas – 2018 Christian Indie Award Winner

When sabotage threatens the Rudin Sugar Factory, Detective Jasper Hollock believes this will be his first real case. But dear Mr. Rudin—the only father Jasper has ever known—holds a different assignment for his private investigator. Mr. Rudin charges Jasper to build a "case" of reasons for his employer to continue his life. If he fails, Mr. Rudin will end it in suicide on Christmas night.

As the incidents at the factory become life threatening, Jasper's attempts at dissuading Mr. Rudin prove futile, and Jasper is left staring at the stark reality of his own soul. Time is ticking. Jasper must solve both cases by Christmas before Mr. Rudin, the company, and Jasper's faith, are dragged to perdition. Will this be the Christmas Jasper truly discovers what makes life worth living?

12 Sisters Who Changed History

Photo Credits:

"Mattei Athena" [Public domain], via Wikimedia Commons
Athens coin picture By cgb.fr [CC BY-SA 3.0
(https://creativecommons.org/licenses/by-sa/3.0)], via Wikimedia Commons.
Amphora birth Athena: Louvre Museum [Public domain], from Wikimedia
Commons
The goddess Diana - Louvre Museum [Public domain], via Wikimedia Commons
Ephesian Coin depicting Diana. By cgb.fr [CC BY-SA 3.0
(https://creativecommons.org/licenses/by-sa/3.0)], via Wikimedia Commons
Fresco of Rachel Weeping By Unknown - Macedonian Encyclopedia, MANU,
2009, p., Public Domain,
https://commons.wikimedia.org/w/index.php?curid=32385228
Fresco by Giovanni Battista Tiepolo of Rachel sitting on the **idols**. Public
domain.
Dante's Vision of Rachel and Leah – **Dante Gabriel Rossetti**, 1855 By Tate
Gallery, online database: entry N05228, Public Domain
Rachel is weeping for her children, 14th century fresco from **Marko's
Monastery**.By Unknown - Macedonian Encyclopedia, MANU, 2009, p., Public
Domain, https://commons.wikimedia.org/w/index.php?curid=32385228
Tru'ng Sisters Statue in **Ho Chi Minh City** CC BY-SA 3.0,
https://en.wikipedia.org/w/index.php?curid=25279954
Procession of elephants in the Trưng Sisters' Parade in Saigon, 1957 By Press and
Information Office, Embassy of the Republic of Vietnam - Press and Information
Office, Embassy of the Republic of Vietnam, Public Domain,
https://commons.wikimedia.org/w/index.php?curid=6592007
Mary Boleyn By Unknown - http://tudorhistory.org/people/mboleyn/, Public
Domain, **https://commons.wikimedia.org/w/index.php?curid=213847**
Anne Boleyn By anonymous -
http://www.siue.edu/~ejoy/eng208lecturenotessonnets.htm (see also National
Portrait Gallery, London: NPG 668), Public Domain,
https://commons.wikimedia.org/w/index.php?curid=1283649
Woodcutting of the Execution of Anne Boleyn, Public Domain
Young Elizabeth I By wartburg.edu, Public Domain,
https://commons.wikimedia.org/w/index.php?curid=686176
English coins, public domain from National Numismatic Collection, National
Museum of American History.
Elizabeth I Darnley Portrait, Public Domain
Young Mary Tudor By Master John (floruit 1544-1545) - Scanned from the book
The National Portrait Gallery History of the Kings and Queens of England by
David Williamson, ISBN 1855142287., Public Domain,
https://commons.wikimedia.org/w/index.php?curid=6640332
Maria Tudor I 1553, Public Domain
Sarah Grimke By Unknown, Public Domain from Library of Congress
Angelina Grimke By Unknown, Public Domain from Library of Congress

www.ingramcontent.com/pod-product-compliance
Lightning Source LLC
Chambersburg PA
CBHW050439010526
44118CB00013B/1594